THOUGHT WATCHERS

DEVELOPING THE INNER MAN TO CONQUER THE FLESH

Bishop M.B. Jefferson

Publisher: Scripture Music Group LLC
805 E Bloomingdale Avenue
Brandon, Florida 33511
mbjeffersonministries.org

Credits:
Cover Designer/ Graphics: Joseph Anthony
Layout/ Editor: Cynthia Ahmed

Your respect and support for this author is much appreciated.
NOTE: *All Scriptures cited in this book are from the King James Version of the Bible unless otherwise noted.*

Library of Congress Control Number: 2021906576
ISBN: 978-1-7365465-3-6

ACKNOWLEDGMENTS

I thank God for all of you reading this book.

I want to acknowledge my loving wife, Dr. Brenda Jefferson. Thank you for helping me honey, I appreciate your words of wisdom and faithfulness. You help me make the impossible possible, each and every day.

To all of my sons and daughters, both spiritual and in the natural, your support means the world to me and I pray this book continues to guide you and gives you wisdom on your walk with God.

A special thank you to all of the Overseer's & Ministers of W.A.F.I (World Assemblies Fellowship International), Pastor Calvin, and Pastor Ninkia on always going the extra mile.

Thought Watchers

TABLE OF CONTENTS

Thought Watchers

INTRODUCTION

Every day I discover more about God and His capacity for miracles. On my journey to know Him, He reveals Himself to me more and more. In my seventy plus years in ministry, I have been strengthened every step of the way, through His Word. I have always had a gift and insight for uncovering the Scriptures, keeping my mind focused on Heavenly things has been a practical tool for me to combat the lies of the enemy and the negativity of *this* world.

I am a part of this world, but my home is in Heaven. I am a sojourner, passing through, ministering, and striving to help others along the way. **Follow me, as I follow Christ.**

The principles embraced in this book are practical ways to conquer everyday obstacles. Everyone has a story. My story began as a troubled youth in Dallas, Texas to eventually becoming a night watchman in Vietnam, to later ministering in Tampa, Florida. If I would have known all the things that I know now, a lot of events wouldn't have happened to me. If I would have had the revelation of being a *'thought watcher'* back then, I certainly would not have encountered many of the hardships that made manifest in my life.

In reading on, I hope to give you insight on the troubles of the flesh and offer wisdom to help you overcome any personal struggles in your own life.

Thought Watchers

Being ordained for ministry, I could not prevent the suffering, persecution, and hardship that I've had to endure over the years. It made me who I am today. Yet, those experiences revealed first-hand to me, what being attacked from demonic forces consists of. I would wake up in the middle of the night sweating, my heart beating fast from visions of a car turning over and over. Over and over, and then out comes a little baby. Then, another child and another child.

At the time, I didn't know what was going on in these visions. Eventually, God showed me that if I would have been watching my thoughts, I would have never gotten caught up in adultery, fornication, and lust. In my heart, I didn't want to do those things, but that stronghold that kept me bound was so intense, that I just couldn't get free. Don't be deceived, you *can* make mistakes and you *can* do wrong if you are not watching your thoughts. I'm a living witness! When I look back, I am so grateful that He kept me. I thank God that He delivered me from my sins.

Being amongst fellow believers and confessing salvation, will not prevent temptation. For example, I was in the church and I was saved, but it took me years for God to bring me out of what I was going through. Don't get it twisted! Saved and unsaved people *can* commit sin until they learn to control their thoughts. Through God we can overcome, He gives us the power over everything around us, through the Scriptures. Everything is subject to the Word of God.

I am convinced that if you are watching your thoughts, nothing can touch you. Lust can't overpower you. Addiction can't take hold of you. Through the mind, God enables us to overcome addiction and sin. Through the mind, we can change the world that we live in, changing our circumstances for better or for worse. "Behold I give unto you power to tread on serpents and scorpions, and over all the power of the enemy: and nothing shall by any means hurt you," (Lk. 10:19).

The enemy would constantly try to manipulate and torment my mind. I remember sitting up in Dallas, Texas and something grabbing hold of me. All of a sudden, I would find myself getting dressed to tip-toe to this woman's house or that woman. My flesh leading me further and further into sin. That lust spirit attached itself to me everywhere I went, from Dallas, TX to Tampa, FL. Developing *my* inner man has been a process of trial and error, making strides and falling short, God's deliverance and His mercy. I would pray at night and repent in my heart, all to get caught up and do those things all over again.

Even through my shortcomings, I still knew that God had a calling on my life. Since a young adult, God would reveal Himself to me little by little. As a toddler, I was introduced to death firsthand with the loss of my six month old baby sister. Then, as a young child, I struggled with alcoholism and addiction at seven years old. I would find cigarettes to inhale from ash trays, getting into this and that. My troublesome curiosity wandering wild. Later, the spirit of lust overtook me and had a ripple effect on my mind. I needed the Holy Spirit to heal *my* spirit and teach me how to control my thoughts.

Returning home from the war, I sought to escape the echoes of gun flashes and horrific memories, often drowning myself in the pleasures of alcohol, women and marijuana. High as a Georgia-pine, I would go from this place to that place and from this woman to that woman. I would wake up to a mysterious tune, singing to myself, "Gotta find a ho! Gotta find a ho." So many women, I couldn't even rest at night. I would be behind the pulpit preaching and ministering, laying hands and helping others get delivered, all while thinking in my mind, "When God?... How about me?"

I knew that abiding in God's Spirit and His Word, was the only way for me to stay on the straight and narrow path that He had for me. Thank God I was ordained to be delivered, but in my own strength I was unable to break the habit. In my own power, I would hit rock bottom every time. "I am the vine, ye are the branches: He that abideth in me, and I in him, the same bringeth forth much fruit: for without me ye can do nothing," (Jn. 15:5). The moment I really knew I had to change was when I had an experience with death and God put a light in me. God had to overthrow my plans and shatter my pattern. He knew that in order to stop the cycle, He had to send something significant to get my attention.

Bishop M.B. Jefferson

I'm thankful! Nevertheless, how many people out there just can't get free? How many people in the world want to be delivered and just don't know how? Many people think that we are simply destined to go to Heaven. Yes, sure you may make it to Heaven, but not without a fight. Trust me. It's a cross that all of us had to bare. I am revealing to you what led me to the Scriptures. I am sharing my own personal cross, in hopes that it will spark a light within you. This wicked cross that I carried was heavy, but thank God for Jesus Christ. Thank God for His precious blood shed on calvary. A supernatural healing power and true deliverance can be found in watching your thoughts and following Him. "And He said to them all, if any man will come after me, let him deny himself, and take up his cross daily, and follow me," (Lk. 9:23).

Take responsibility for where you are in your life. Become a thought watcher and ask God to transform you from the inside-out. Let your *cross* be a positive one, reflecting the light of Christ. Do good, by bringing in souls into His House. Minister to others and preach the gospel without fear. In the flesh, we are unable to please God. **No good thing dwells outside of the spirit.** We must elevate our thinking and stand on guard, watching the gates of our mind. Pray and be mindful to observe, then after you observe - you must do. I wasn't always living right, but my hope is that my testimony will bring someone closer to Him. That someone will want to know about this man who changed my life. *Have you heard of this man called, Jesus?*

Thought Watchers

If you watch your thoughts, soon you will find yourself unable to commit sin. If you guard the gates of your mind, sin will have no place in you. You have to pull that specific stronghold down, whether it is lust, or lying, or backbiting. Pull it down. Cast it down, then capture it and bring it under God's will. Control that "high thing" that tries to come against the knowledge of God. Remind yourself, that the devil is under your feet.

I challenge you to begin today. It will take focus. It will not happen overnight. I am not telling you it will be easy. Be prepared for a fight when you start watching the matters of your mind. For some, it takes them years and years to come out of all the junk they have gotten themselves into. Seek God and stand in the Holy place. By controlling your thoughts, you have the supernatural ability to control your Spirit. Soon, like breathing – it will become natural to you.

If you want to do what's right and you're doing what is wrong, you will find it bothering you, plaguing your mind, over and over again. It will continue to bother you until you make a change. It will continue to bother you until you make up your mind, to let Him in. All God is saying to you today is become a **thought watcher**.

Sin can be devastating sometimes. It wasn't until I lay convulsing on a hospital bed at twenty-five years old, that God opened my eyes to the reality of sin, Hell, and death. Being incapacitated, it took numerous doctors to try and revive me from an acute allergic reaction. My heart stopped for seconds. Beep. Beep. **Beeepppp.** The doctors called it. Not knowing, in that moment I was traveling down a dark tunnel, screaming at the top of my lungs "I don't want to die, someone please save me." It wasn't until several minutes later, that I woke up startled by the faces of the concerned doctors around me.

God had given me another chance. From that moment, my life was forever changed. From that moment forward, I began the journey of becoming a thought watcher.

After my life-altering experience, I shared my story and soon received a license in the mail that said *minister*. This gesture touched my heart and God began to deal with me. You can confess salvation all day long, but only the power of God, and keeping your mind stayed on Him can truly impact your life. Lust doesn't go away by simply praising God. It's there and you know it's there, but unless God delivers you, there isn't much you can do about it. If you are trying to do it on your own, it's not going to work. Getting rid of *it* in your own efforts won't make it disappear. That's what many call trying to 'do it on your own,' or your own self-righteousness. It took me years, but God gave me the grace not to give up. Whatever you are going through, I want to encourage you today - don't give up! You keep fighting and keep fighting. Eventually, with God's help, it will go away. It has to go away, because God has ordained you for life.

Devils are territorial. The enemy wants you to stay in your same predicament. Oh, but when God got me! I knew it. You can be in sin and needing deliverance, but still believe God for your freedom. If you belong to God, you've got to fight.

I remember, I was casting out devils, "walking the water" and everything else, but lust was still there. You can proclaim salvation and still do wrong. You can abstain for a month or two months, but to truly be delivered means you don't do it again. That desire actually leaves you because you don't want that spirit anymore. Your mind and your heart no longer want that weight of sin. The weight of sin is heavy. God can warn you and warn you, until eventually He will hold you accountable.

Thought watchers have learned, through God, to watch their thoughts. You must fight contrary thoughts away from you. It's not an hour prayer, it's not a sixty-second prayer, thought watchers must watch day and night. Night and day. When you get up in the morning, things cross your mind. When you go to get some water at night, something else crosses your mind. You have to take that mind and make sure it is always in tune with God. Stay encouraged, as you fight the good fight of faith.

Thought watchers are different than anybody else, they are constantly watching their thoughts. I have learned through God to become aware of my mindset. This is not a momentary reflection of casting down imaginations for an hour, but night and day. Day and night, twenty-four seven we must cast down any imaginations and resist any temptations from the enemy. The enemy is out to destroy you. You must take control of your mind. Make sure your mind is always aligned with God and stay in His Word. Come out of the flesh by overcoming temptation.

Eventually, I learned that the ministry most preachers have, is often conducive of what they went through in their lives. What was once your cross, becomes your tool, or token to help other people who have the same problem. All things are manifest by light. "But all things that are reproved are made manifest by the light: for whatsoever doth make manifest is light. Wherefore He saith, Awake though that sleepest, and arise from the dead, and Christ shall give thee light," (Eph. 5:13-14).

Across the nation, I am humbled to teach ministers and help those who need deliverance. My trials and testimonies have allowed me to be a vessel, to show other people the way to Jesus. My prayer is that the wisdom given in this book, will help someone else draw closer to Him. Deliverance comes through the Word of God.

Deliver your mind from the hands of the enemy by becoming a thought watcher. To overcome the flesh and live your life in *His Spirit*, you must take action now and redeem the days. Arise from slumber and recognize the signs of the times. The days are evil. God is closer now than He has ever been before. God is giving you the grace to not give up. *Will you commit to watching your thoughts?*

Will you make a change today?

Thought Watchers

1 BEGGING TO BE DELIVERED

Think of a time when you drove through various areas in your local city, or traveled around the country. *What did you see?* In these instances, you may have seen people walking, crossing the street, shopping for groceries, eating at a restaurant, or conversing on a park bench. Everybody moving around in solidarity, yet with a different purpose in mind. Looking about, we see strangers who we do not know. As interesting as these individual's stories may seem, as intriguing as their agenda is, we cannot know them in passing or driving by. We cannot understand the inside narrative of their lives from the outside looking in. Many people are well put together and functioning in everyday life, but desperately struggling with addiction or sin in their innermost parts. In times like these, so many people are privately begging God for deliverance. Let's travel through the pages and take a look at their stories.

In the city somewhere, there is a young woman is in a run-down motel room, staring at the crumbling walls in shame. Too empty to even look at herself in the mirror. She glances over at the dingy

1

dresser and the small bit of money she received after offering her body to a paying customer. In disgust, she muffles a cry silently so her partner or 'pimp' outside the door cannot hear her.

She begins to clench her hands close to her, as she mentally prepares for her next appointment. Rocking back and forth, she begins to think of what it would be like to be free. She's heard of God but doesn't really know Him. She is not sure who would even listen if she asked for help. Inwardly, she prays for the strength to stop and the courage to change her life. In her pain and regret, she holds her face in her hands, looking down at the floor. She doesn't know what to do. She begins to whisper a prayer, *begging to be heard, begging to be delivered.*

Driving further down, across town there is a man limping because the soles of his feet are intensely blistered. He has been walking around for days, with no sleep and with holes in the bottom of his shoe. His big toe scraping the ground with each step. Finally, reaching his destination he passes through the smoke of a crowded crack house, moving through sexually suggestive women, stepping over people passed out on the floor. He knocks on a door to pay the man who will give him his next fix. He is hungry and has no place to go, yet all he can think of is getting high. His wife and children have given up hope. After numerous attempts at recovery, his addiction leads him to wander into abandon houses and to inject a fluid into his veins, hoping to ease his ache. He has lost so much weight; his

2

skeleton is barely supporting his skin. Yet, at night he looks up from the contaminated mattress and out of the broken window to the night sky. He closes his eyes and prays silently to himself for the ability to stop, for the ability to get clean and come home to his family. Inwardly, he is *begging God to be delivered.*

A few blocks down the road, mischief lurks. Underneath an empty bridge, an uncompromising dealer gives one last warning, one last request for his drug money from a distraught buyer. The remorseful man before him is on his knees shaking, back turned, hands tied, and is pleading for his life. The gangsters at the rear of the dealer are straight-faced, armed and dressed in all-black. They champion the dealer's retribution and all stand in wait to make the man "pay".

The notorious supplier gives the debtor one last opportunity to save his life. In response to his inability to deliver, he lifts his Glock 19 to the temple of his face and without hesitation, pulls the trigger. Boom! It's done. The abrupt sound echoes throughout the rain. Then, silence. Blood pools around his lifeless body, when the dealer turns and walks away. That night, he lets the shower run longer than usual to wash the blood off of his body. Under the water, he looks at his blood stained hands and masks his tears in the stream. On the outside, he's a stone-cold killer, but on the inside, he is tired of hurting other people. He is tired of living this way. He does not know how much longer he can continue to do this. He is *begging God to be delivered.*

Miles away, down the interstate and across state lines, there is a teenager in the self-checkout line at a store. She is carrying a basket full of feminine items, make-up, some food and a few late-night snacks. Her mother told her to go down to the corner store and bring home some milk. She has been trying to find ways to fill her idle time, getting involved in various petty crimes to feel wanted. She knows better, but her father is always working. Her mom is always busy with the T.V. remote and a bottle. In fact, her new friends seem to support her new habit.

So like clockwork, she walks over to scan the pieces of merchandise, being sure to cover the barcode of the expensive items and puts them quickly in the bag. She walks out the shop inconspicuously and disappears from the store camera, as if nothing ever happened. When the young girl gets home, she hands her mother the receipt and puts the milk in the fridge. Goes up to her room and slops in her bed, then begins to think over her actions. While acting cold and indifferent, on the inside she is regretful. She starts to cry uncontrollably wondering why she can't stop shoplifting. No one sees her. No one in her family knows what she is struggling with. Yet, she cries out to God *begging to be delivered.*

So many people today are hurting. If we drive further up the coast, there is mother in her beautiful Victorian home, preparing

4

lunch for her three kids as they head off to school. She kisses her husband as he heads to work, waves goodbye as they start their morning and shuts the door. Up the stairs, she opens her dresser. Then, begins digging under the drawer for her secret stash. She picks up an unlabeled pill bottle, twists the cap, and takes more than the recommended dose of her *non-prescription* drug to calm her nerves. Her thoughts wander and her feelings suddenly become numb. She silently debates whether to tell her husband or family of her addiction. She is not sure if she is suicidal or just depressed. With her Bible at her bedside, the kids have no idea that their *perfect* mom has a persistent problem. All of a sudden, she bursts out in tears and decides to discard the rest of the pills down the toilet. Watching her secret obsession swirl down the drain, she sits on the cold bathroom floor, make-up smudged by her tears and starts to pray. She *begins to beg God for freedom, begging God to be delivered.*

On a regular basis, people are asking how to get victory over sin in their lives. In all of these scenarios, we cannot see these individual's thoughts or iniquities. Like the people in passing, they each have an individual battle with the flesh or a trial to overcome. Their struggles consist of tiers of issues, their insecurities, and hardships. Yet only God can see into a person's heart, know their thoughts, and can deliver them from sin. "They know not, neither will they understand; they walk on in darkness: all of the foundations of the Earth are out of course. I have said, Ye are gods; and all of you are children of the most High, but ye shall die like men, and fall like one of the princes," (Psa. 82:5-7).

Some people overcome their flesh, then they make progress and go right back into doing wrong *again*. Some non-believers don't see "it" as transgression, but are simply tired of living the lifestyle they are in. Whatever your specific situation may be today, to truly be free, you have to make up in your mind that you no longer want to do wrong. Watch what you are thinking and watch what you are saying to yourself. You must command your body and your mind to submit to the Spirit of God. English minister, John Owen once said, "There is no way of deliverance from the state and condition of being in the flesh, but by the Spirit of Christ."

Overall, those who may be strangers in passing; even those associates and friends you may know, fight silent battles with the flesh each and every day. The good news is that God hears your plea. He is patient and merciful to help all of us. He will not leave you feeling empty, God will get right down there in the trenches with you to help. If you are unable to stop doing wrong, this is an indication that you are thinking the wrong thoughts. "For whosoever shall keep the whole law, and yet offend in one point, he is guilty of all," (Jam. 2:10).

Ultimately, our days are determined by one of two driving forces – the flesh or the Spirit. **It *is* possible to control what is trying to control you.** You aren't meant for the flesh to rule your life – you're meant to walk in the spirit and live life on a higher level, where victory reigns and righteousness rules. Anything that is out of line with the Word of God is a hindrance. Allow the Holy Spirit to correct and guide you, as you work towards walking in the Spirit every day. "Wherefore seeing we also are compassed about with so great a cloud of witnesses, let us lay aside every weight, and the sin which doth so easily beset us, and let us run with patience the race that is set before us," (Heb. 12:1).

God wants us to get to the point where we no longer strive against sin. We need to get to the point where we desire the things of God more than anything else, separating ourselves from the lusts of the world. If you don't give God time throughout your day, natural temptations will overwhelm you and this is how most people get off track.

Laying aside the things of the world means giving up activities, friends, and habits that don't match God's best for our lives. "Ye did run well; who did hinder you that you should not obey the truth? This persuasion cometh not of him that calleth you. A little leaven leaveneth the whole lump. I have confidence in you through the Lord, that you will be none otherwise minded: but he that troubleth you shall bear his judgment, whosoever he be," (Gal. 5:7-10). **Take heart, you can be free today.**

An inevitable chain of events will unfold when you do not think before you act. Sin will unfold when you engage in evil works, it starts in the mind. These transgressions manifest afterwards, as things that make you feel unhappy, things you know you don't want to do, but can't seem to stop. American evangelical author, Kevin DeYoung once said, "The reason for your entire salvation, the design behind your deliverance, the purpose for which God chose you in the first place is Holiness."

There is an answer to every problem you're facing today — whether it be petitioning to overcome addiction, sin, financial strain, health, or family-related circumstances. **If you are seeking freedom from sin, ask God to give you a repentant heart.** Likewise, if you are already a believer, ask God to open your mind to feel what other people may be going through. Then, be merciful. There is a man or a woman roaming the streets, digging through filth to look for a morsel of bread or a piece of fruit out of the trash today. Someone is wondering how they are going to put food on the table for their children, after losing their job. Another may be scrounging for change to pay a hotel bill, to prevent them from sleeping in their car.

Recognize your transgression, watch your thoughts, ask God to deliver you, and repent! "But the fearful and unbelieving, and the abominable, and murderers, and whoremongers, and sorcerers, and idolaters, and all liars, shall have their part in the lake which burneth with fire and brimstone: which is the second death," (Rev. 21:8). Don't be ashamed to ask for help, don't be timid to plead for your cause, God can deliver you from destruction. He can help you overcome the flesh and strengthen your inner-man.

Lay your burdens down. Walk in the Spirit of God and you will not fulfill the lusts of the flesh. **Laying aside these contrary ideas and persuasions require us to watch our thoughts.**

Everything in life is built off of God, make Him the center focus of your life. "(7) Let the wicked forsake his way, and the unrighteous man his thoughts: and let him return unto the Lord, and He will have mercy upon him; and to our God, He will abundantly pardon. (8) For my thoughts are not your thoughts, neither are your ways my ways, saith the Lord. (9) For as the Heavens are higher than the Earth, so are my ways higher than your ways, and my thoughts than your thoughts," (Isa. 55:7-9).

An individual can be sorry for misdeeds. They can even show sorrow, guilt, or conviction but true repentance is needed to experience deliverance. Then, salvation is a result of that confession, repentance, and deliverance from sin. "And I will deliver thee out of the hand of the wicked, and I will redeem thee out of the hand of the terrible," (Jer. 15:21).

Once God sets you free, stay free! There will always be temptation, and this is where learning how to live in the Spirit of God takes precedence. *We must learn to live in the flesh but not operate according to the flesh.* "Now unto Him that is able to do exceeding abundantly above all that we ask or think, according to the power that worketh in us," (Eph. 3:20).

Ask God to move in your Spirit. Sensing God's movement in our heart is called revelation and discernment. Lifestyle changes are a result of focus, action, and prayer. Discern the right path to take. Ask God to reveal the right thoughts to think and the right words to speak. To walk in righteous thinking, we must focus on it and intentionally practice it, until it becomes a natural and instinctive part of our life.

In working to overcome the flesh, often we neglect the Spirit. Many times we focus so intensely on *not* making an error, that we miss intentionally focusing on living life and doing good. Build up yourself by praying in the Holy Ghost and focus on what gives your Spirit life. "But the fruit if the Spirit is love, joy, peace, longsuffering, gentleness, goodness, faith, meekness, temperance, against such there is no law," (Gal. 5:22-23). The foundation of Holiness can only be laid by Jesus Christ. Freedom to walk unashamed, healed, redeemed, and happy is found through Jesus. "Who hath delivered us from the power of darkness, and hath translated us into the kingdom of His dear son," (Col. 1:13). Let the redeemed of the Lord, say so!

As a *'thought watcher,'* deliverance belongs to you. You don't need to beg God for what He willingly wants to give you, which is an abundant life, hope and happiness. In salvation, you can rejoice because your name is written in the book of life. **As thought watchers, we must all become WORD-CONSCIOUS.** Peace comes from being spiritual-minded. "The Lord rewarded me according to my righteousness; according to the cleanness of my hands hath He recompensed me," (Psa. 18:20).

A spiritual-minded person becomes a direct representation of the voice of God, they can control everything, because Word of God controls the universe. Love God with all your heart and build off of the solid foundation which is Christ. Walk in freedom today.

My Chapter Notes:

_____

_____

_____

_____

_____

_____

Thought Watchers

Reference Scriptures:

Psalm 18.20

Psalm 82:5-7

Isaiah 55:7-9

Jeremiah 15:21

Galatians 5:7-10

Galatians 5:22-23

Ephesians 3:20

Colossians 1:13

Hebrews 12:1

James 2:10

Revelations 21:8

2 TEMPTATION AND THE WORKS OF THE FLESH

Has a thought ever crossed your mind that you couldn't explain? Have you ever doubted a decision? Maybe hesitated in taking on a new task or pursuing a desire? Daily, we have various images in the media and people in our lives striving to motivate us, grabbing for our attention, seeking to direct our focus and actions. We must be mindful of the 'matters of our mind' and the temptations that seek to connect with our Spirit, doing this we can overcome the flesh and overcome wrong thinking.

Thoughts are constantly impacting our daily decisions and choices. Whether you contemplate buying a boat or a car, after scrolling online and seeing an ad. Or if you contemplate pulling over after leaving the gym, having glanced at an image of a burger in bright lights on a billboard. Maybe even avoiding the hasty urge to buy a dress, that the window manikin so stylishly wears. The media and marketing are always seeking to tempt our flesh with carnal desires. Advertisers depend on our desires, weaknesses, and impulses to boost profit by constantly grabbing for our attention, as many unknowingly clicking "add to cart."

The works of the flesh comes in many forms. Perhaps, you wanted to say some 'not so nice' words or phrases that came to mind when a stranger skipped you in line at the store. Or had the nerve to steal your parking space while you waited patiently and had your blinker on. As a youth, did you ever considered sneaking out to the school dance, in spite of your parent's objection? Or considered hiding in the bathroom to sneak a moment alone to get high or smoke? **The truth is that many people have difficulty resisting temptation at least occasionally, even if what tempts them differs.**

Let's think about it.

How many times have you been sound asleep in the middle of the night and been awoken by the sudden urge for something sweet? Conceivably a carton of night-time ice cream. Or you suddenly want to binge on a twinkie. You experience a hasty urge or desire in your physical body to eat – even though you may have had dinner just a few hours before. Your head may ache or your mouth water, until you give in to this tasty seduction. Of course, you listen to your belly. With each bite, you indulge and smile content. Yet, moments after to feel bloated, uncomfortably full and grimacing with guilt.

It started in the garden.

We can collectively imagine that this is just how Adam and Eve must have felt after eating the fruit that changed the course of humanity. "(1) Now the serpent was more subtil than any beast of the field which the Lord God had made. And he said unto the woman, Yea, hath God said, Ye shall not eat of every tree of the garden? (5) For God doth know that in the day ye eat thereof, then your eyes shall be opened, and ye shall be as gods, knowing good and evil," (Gen. 3:1,5). Similarly, **temptation** is the urge to fulfill a want; something that causes a strong desire to have or do something, especially something that is bad, wrong, or unwise. It is defined as a cause or occasion of enticement. Likewise, that infamous 'fruit' of the garden symbolizes seduction, sin, and temptation.

"(7) And the eyes of both of them were opened, and they knew that they were naked; and they sewed fig leaves together, and made themselves aprons. (8)...and Adam and his wife hid themselves from the presence of the Lord God amongst the trees of the garden. (10)...[Adam said] I was afraid, because I was naked, and I hid myself. (12)... [Saying] the woman who thou gavest to be with me, she gave me of the tree, and I did eat. (13)...And the woman [diverted responsibility saying], the serpent beguiled me, and I did eat," (Gen. 3:7-13).

Ultimately, God cursed the ground because they did wrong. "(16) Unto the woman He said, I will greatly multiply thy sorrow and thy conception; in sorrow thou shalt bring forth children; and thy desire shall be to thy husband, and he shall rule over thee. (17) And unto Adam He said, because thou hast hearkened unto the voice of thy wife, and hast eaten of the tree, of which I command thee, saying, Thou shalt not eat of it: cursed is the ground for thy sake; in sorrow shalt thou eat of it all they days of thy life," (Gen. 3:14-19). This one decision, this one moment of weakness where they acted in disobedience altered their lives, and the destiny of generations to come. Unfortunately, all of human nature was founded upon this innate desire for pleasurable things.

Even so, actions have after-effects.

What would you do, if you knew the outcome of your actions ahead of time? For example, imagine a fictional scenario of being given the opportunity to predisposition your choices, thoughts and actions. Such as, a time-machine to view the future or past. To have the time and the ability to meditate on your options, prior to making harmful choices that may be bad for you or lead you to an untimely result.

For instance, envision that you could anticipate that being drunk at the bar would lead to you to an accident that evening, or that one more 'hit' of that drug would lead you to a lifetime of addiction, or that small innocent conversation would lead to an abusive or toxic relationship. Given the chance, many would say "No," I would choose right. It's obvious, "I would stop... I would never do that."

However, the lure of sin is never obvious. When Satan comes, he is deceptive and cunning, often being distorted as a false representation of what we want (2 Cor. 11:13-14). Disguised as the snake in the garden, seemingly innocent and presenting goodwill advice. "But I fear, lest by any means, as the serpent beguiled Eve through subtility, so your minds should be corrupted from the simplicity that is in Christ. For if he that cometh preacheth another Jesus, whom we have not preached, or if ye receive another spirit, which ye have not received, or another gospel, which ye have not accepted, ye might well bear with him," (2 Cor. 11:3-4). It is because of this self-regulation failure that we are constantly reminded of our desperate need for God. In our own minds, we are easily deceived, confused, and lost (Matt. 24:24). We need the truth of His Word to help us daily and wise-counsel to guide us in our decision-making.

While we can't predict the future, or travel to undo regrets of the past in real life, we can surrender to a Savior who is greater than any seduction of sin. We can become aware of our desires and wants; developing a deep understanding of the Word of God and how to navigate through life, operating based on the inner-man. As you move towards controlling your natural desires and submitting to God, you become one step closer to conquering your flesh.

All throughout Scripture, the word **flesh** is used to describe sinful tendencies and carnal sins. *Carne* is the Spanish word for "meat," to live after the things that animals live for. In the Greek translation, 'sarkikos' or carnal is tied to the idea of uncontrolled behavior. In a sense, Paul was describing human nature as primal. When operating in the flesh, we are acting out animal-like cravings and instincts, as a result of not using the mind of Christ or following God to make better decisions. "For who hath known the mind of the Lord, that he may instruct him? But we have the mind of Christ," (1 Cor. 2:16). If a shark is hungry, it takes a bite. If a scorpion is triggered, it stings! If a lion sees that you are running, it will chase you. These are natural "primal" instincts that an animal cannot control.

Are you allowing God to be in control? Are you watching your thoughts? Do you react based on your primal urges? Or are you truly operating in the Spirit?

We often associate 'the world,' the flesh, and the devil as the sources of temptation to sin. Yet, there is nothing more harmful than our own unguarded thoughts. "It is the spirit that quickeneth: the flesh profiteth nothing, the words that I speak unto you, they are spirit, and they are life," (Jn. 6:63). *Quicken* means to make alive, to revive; to stimulate or cause to burn more intensely. God blew into the dust of the ground creating Adam. The breath of God is a representation of the Spirit of God. "And the Lord God formed man from the dust of the ground, and breathed into his nostrils the breath of life; and man became a living soul," (Gen. 2:7).

Are you living the life God intended you to live? The Holy Spirit changes our desires and manifests Christ in you the hope of glory

(Col. 1:27). Only the Holy Spirit has the power to make the changes that God wants to make in our lives. The inner man has to arise. Shake yourself and say, 'Wake up!' It's a new day and Christ is here to set you free. "(27) Woe unto you, scribes and Pharisees, hypocrites! For ye are like unto whited sepulchres, which indeed appear beautiful outward, but are within full of dead men's bones, and all of uncleanness. (28) Even so ye also outwardly appear righteous unto me, but within ye are full of hypocrisy and iniquity," (Matt. 23:27-28). God looks at the heart, He sees and cares about your thoughts and intentions. The inner man reveals who we are. God looks on inside of a person, at the inside on those things which are unseen (1 Sam. 16:7).

If we achieve Earthly success and material gain, with a comfortable bank account, and a refrigerator full of food, an investment of gold and jewelry, luxury furniture and the best education, fulfilling gratification after gratification of the flesh; **in the end *we all* still perish**. Having *every* beautiful woman or handsome man, trying *every* drug or indulgence in liquor, being angry and acting out every impulse will never satisfy the emptiness in your heart. What you are truly feeling... that hole in your heart is a deep abyss of sin and it is making you spiritually sick. French music composer, Oliver Messiaen once said, "The human being is flesh and consciousness, body and soul; his heart is an abyss which can only be filled by that which is Godly." Being righteous is a conscious decision to stay in the faith and grow in God. Being double-minded is a sickness of the inner man. "The full soul loatheth a honeycomb; but to the hungry soul every bitter thing is sweet," (Prov. 27:7).

The hamster wheel in the 'pursuit of happiness' never ends, it's a circle that goes around and around; and it's never enough. There is a cold tomb and judgement waiting for us all and how we live our lives on this side, will determine our ability to see God and reach Heaven in the next (Rom. 8:5-8). From dust we came, and to dust we will return. "For what is a man profited, if he shall gain the whole world, and lose his own soul? Or what shall a man give in exchange for his soul?" (Matt. 16:26).

The spirit or soul are defined as the part of an individual which partakes in divinity or damnation; as believers we deem it to survive the death of the body. However, where the spirit goes is based on our daily choices, decisions, and actions. "Hell and destruction are never full, so the eyes of man are never satisfied," (Prov. 27:20).

In order to make a change, in order to stop operating in the works of the flesh, we must examine ourselves. **Take account of what you have done, are doing, and want to do.** Then, see how many times you have tried to stop? What worked? What didn't work? "(14) For we know that the law is spiritual: but I am carnal, sold under sin. (15) For that which I do, I allow not: for what I would, that do I not; but what I hate, that I do... (18) For I know that in me (that is, in my flesh,) dwelleth no good thing: for to will is present with me; but how to perform that which I find good I find not," (Rom. 7:14-18).

Even if you may not desire to act on your emotions or lust, bear in mind, nonetheless that you must bring your own members, mind, and body under subjection to God. Your body is the temple of God. Whether you participate in acts of gluttony (over-indulgence in food), drug and alcohol abuse, excess lust by sexual gratification, viewing pornography, or simply over-spending; it is a type of transgression. This sin against yourself and against God is hindering your blessings. "(19) For the good that I would I do not: but the evil which I would not, that I do. (20) Now if I do that I would not, it is no more I that do it, but sin that dwelleth in me... (22) For I delight in the law of God after the *inward* man," (Rom. 7:19-22). Be committed to present your bodies as a living sacrifice, Holy and acceptable to God.

In these times of national affliction and crisis, God is testing the whole world. However, He is testing the believers first. Often, sending a strong delusion that some essentially believe a lie. As His children we are not exempt, judgment must begin at the House of God (1 Pet. 4:17). Sin cannot desire *you* unless something is in you. Do right! Look in the mirror. **Then, ask yourself: "Who am I really? Is there anything evil running around in me? What am I doing that I shouldn't be doing?"** Take a moment to examine yourself. What do you *want* from God? What do you *need* Him to help you with?" The flesh and the spirit may be at war, but Jesus is the living water (Gal. 5:16-17). When you come to Him, know that He has already won the battle; He cannot fail you. He will help you. Cast your burdens on Him, He will sustain you.

Practical tools to examine yourself:

- Recognize your tendency to sin
- Flee from temptation
- Resist temptation with the Word of Truth
- Re-focus your mind and heart with praise
- Repent quickly if you make a mistake and start again

The **Works of the Flesh** can be anything that does not please God. In fact, the spirit and the flesh are contrary to one another. There are *three* things which **tempt** us: *the flesh, the world, and the devil.* Do not use your freedom as an occasion to carry out perverse acts in the flesh. In Holiness, we must constrain ourselves, not living secluded and scared to enjoy events, other people, or living in a bubble to 'do no wrong,' but as believers who are aware of Satan's schemes and equipped to resist in any situation. Feed the Spirit, starve the flesh. "...(19) Now the works of the flesh are manifest, which are these, adultery, fornication, uncleanness, lasciviousness. (20) Idolatry, witchcraft, hatred, variance, emulations, wrath, strife, seditions, heresies, (21) envyings, murders, drunkenness, revellings, and such like: of the which I tell you before, as I have also told you in times past, that they which do such things shall not inherit the Kingdom of God...," (Gal. 5:13-26).

In His time here on Earth, Jesus was tempted also.

"Then was Jesus led up of the spirit into the wilderness to be tempted of the devil." He fasted forty days and forty nights, being weak and hungry. In each of the three interactions throughout Matthew 4:1-11, Satan approached Him appealing to what would satisfy His flesh, but Jesus held firm His integrity.

- **Temptation 1 (v3) :** If thou be the Son of God, command that these stones be made bread.
  - o *Jesus' response:* *It is written, Man shall not live by bread alone, but by every word that proceedeth out of the mouth of God.*
- **Temptation 2 (v6) :** If thou be the Son of God, cast thyself down: for it is written, He shall give His angels charge concerning thee, lest at any time thou dash thy foot against a stone.
  - o *Jesus' response:* *It is written, Thou shalt not tempt the Lord thy God.*
- **Temptation 3 (v9) :** (After showing Him the kingdoms of the world and the glory of them). All these things will I give thee, if thou wilt fall down and worship me.

o *Jesus' response:* Get thee hence, Satan: for it is written, Thou shalt worship the Lord thy God, and Him only shalt thou serve.

Our Savior is a powerful example of how to overcome the temptation and testing that comes our way. Since He was tempted as we are, He is able to understand what we face. Jesus could have chosen to use His miraculous power for selfish reasons, however He used it to help and minister to others, and heal to the sick.

In life, we all are tested all the time. The flesh is in direct conflict with the spirit. The flesh demands to be fed; it has an appetite. When the spirit tries to obey, the flesh tries to resist. The flesh has to die, and the inner-man must come alive. If we feed the flesh it will grow, if we feed the spirit it will grow. We feed our spirit through the Word of God, prayer, praise, and Holy communion with Him.

On account of the flesh, an individual is concerned primarily with themselves, to be at the center. *It* is self-seeking and focused on the physical; not concerned with Heavenly things or the inner-man. Ultimately, the flesh is focused on death for it is concerned with time and what is passing away, the body and the world. Too often, the natural wants to be in control. To live according to the flesh you must have your mind set on these natural and carnal desires. Escape, by casting down any thought that do not line up with God's Word (Phil. 4:8, 2 Cor. 10:3-6). The human spirit is focused on light and life. Will

24

you concern yourself with the things of the world or with the things of God? Choose this day who you will serve (Josh. 24:15).

The flesh is as flesh does. A carnal mind cannot comprehend the things of God, it does not grasp spiritual teachings (Rom. 8:7). The flesh is the rebellious, unruly, part of the inner-man. The part of us that does not want to be told what to do. It does not like limits and rules, refuses correction, and does not want to have anything to do with God. It hates to be under authority or to yield to anything other than its own desire. It recoils anything that causes it not to be the center of the universe, the center of primary focus.

It is the part of us attracted by goodness, beauty, and pleasure. Catering to what feels good. The lust of the flesh, the lust of the eye, and the pride of life. "(15) Love not the world, neither the things that are in the world. If any man love the world, the love of the Father is not in him. (16) For all that is in the world, the lust of the flesh, and the lust of the eyes, and the pride of life, is not of the Father, but is of the world. (17) And the world passeth away and the spirit thereof: but he that doeth the will of God abideth forever," (1 Jn. 2:15-17).

Make a decision today to abide in God. A key component of overcoming temptation lies in your ability to resist. To **resist** something is to keep it at bay or to fend off its influence or advance.

- ♦ "Submit yourselves therefore to God. *Resist the devil*, and he will flee from you," (Jam. 4:7).

25

◆ "For the time will come when they will not endure sound doctrine; but after their own lusts shall they heap to themselves teachers, having itching ears; and *they shall turn away* their ears from the truth, and shall be turned unto fables. But watch thou in all things, endure afflictions, do the work of an evangelist, make full proof thy ministry." (2 Tim. 4:3-5).

◆ "But he that sinneth against me wrongeth his own soul: all they that hate me love death," (Prov. 8:36).

◆ "Good understanding giveth favour: but the way of transgressors is hard," (Prov. 13:15).

◆ "Be not overcome of evil, but overcome evil with good," (Rom. 12:21).

◆ "Thy Word have I hid in mine heart, that I *might not* sin against thee," (Psa. 119:11).

◆ "But judgment shall *return unto* righteousness: and all the upright in heart shall follow it," (Psa. 94:15).

◆ "My flesh and my heart faileth: but God is the strength of my heart, and my portion for ever," (Psa. 73:26).

◆ "Even as Sodom and Gomorrha, and the cities about them, in like manner giving themselves over to fornication, and going after strange flesh, are set forth as an example, suffering the vengeance of eternal fire," (Jud. 1:7).

Never give up your desire for change, Stay encouraged! It took me years to overcome my iniquities; from lying to lust, alcohol addiction to having a bad mind. Then, when I overcame one sin, something else would arise that I needed to work on. Thankfully, God set me free! We overcome by the blood of the lamb and the words of our testimony. **Spiritual maturity is a process, however making the decision to _stop_ can happen instantly.** "For therein is the righteousness of God revealed from faith to faith: as it I written, the just shall live by faith," (Rom. 1:17). It's only once *you* have made your mind up that God goes to work on your behalf. Fighting off demons who prey on your weaknesses and helping you resist ungodly strongholds and influences.

Only God can soften the heart of the most hardened criminal. "For God maketh my heart soft, and the Almighty troubleth me," (Job 23:16). Only He can tame the lust of the ladies' man and change the desires of the prostitute. Only He can heal the mind of a murderer and redeem a killer. Only God can clean up the dope fiend and cause him to carry His Word. Only God can make the rich man consider his ways or help the harlot find love. Only God can give wholesome words to the backbiter and cause a liar to tell the truth (Psa. 101:7, Rev. 21:8). Only God can sustain the teen mother and help her live a different way. Only God can help sinners in the way and lead the lost to a path of righteousness (Psa. 25:8). "Can the Ethiopian change his skin, or the leopard his spots? Then may ye also do good, that are accustomed to do evil," (Jer. 13:23).

God sent His own Son to help us to be free from sin, that the law of righteousness might be fulfilled in us. There is no condemnation in what you did in the past, in your weakness, last year or even yesterday. Make a decision *today* to suffer in the flesh for a season; to overcome and conquer your weaknesses (1 Pet. 1:6-7).

The same spirit of Him that raised up Jesus from the dead dwells in you. The inner-man helps our infirmities and makes intercession for us through prayer and speaking in tongues. You are more than a conqueror through Christ. "(6) For to be carnally minded is death; but to be spiritually minded is life and peace... (16) The spirit itself beareth witness with our spirit, that we are the children of God... (37) Nay, in all these things we are more than conquerors through Him that loved us," (Rom. 8:1-39).

God desires our happiness and fulfillment to be found in a life free from fleshly desires, child-like wants, and released from the shackles of sin. **Spiritual wellness is a combination of a healthy mind, body, and spirit.** Health is a state of complete physical, mental and social well-being. Spiritual wellness acknowledges our search for a deeper meaning in life. When we are spiritually healthy, we feel more connected to Christ and more available to help those around us. We have more clarity when it comes to everyday choices, and our actions become more consistent with our beliefs and values. A famous quote from British theologian, Jonathan Edwards says, "The way to Heaven is ascending; we must be content to travel uphill, though it may be hard and tiresome, and contrary to the natural bias of our flesh."

Others may have counted you out, but God will never leave you. Be committed to become what many thought you could not be. Change your lifestyle by developing the inner-man through the Word of God. "For which cause we faint not; but though our outward man perish, the inward man is renewed day by day," (2 Cor. 4:16). Choose not to be entangled again in the yoke of bondage. When you walk in the spirit, you will not fulfill the lust of the flesh. Our inner man, through the power of the Holy Spirit, draws us to desire what is best, what is upright, what is good, and what is helpful.

The Spirit of God is on me to proclaim liberty to you today. Repent! Change your mindset to reflect on God's Word. Allow Christ into your heart. His mercy is available to all of us.

My Chapter Notes:

_____

_____

_____

_____

_____

_____

Reference Scriptures:

Genesis 2:7

Genesis 3:1,5

Genesis 3:7-13

Genesis 3:14-19

Joshua 24:15

1 Samuel 16:7

Job 23:16

Psalm 25:8

Psalm 73:26

Psalm 94:15

Psalm 101:7

Psalm 119:11

Proverbs 8:36

Proverbs 13:15

Proverbs 27:7, 20

Jeremiah 13:23

Matthew 4:1-11

Matthew 16:26

Matthew 23:27-28

Matthew 24:24

John 6:63

Romans 1:17

Romans 7:14-18

Romans 7:19-22

Romans 8:5-8

Romans 8:1-39

Romans 12:21

1 Corinthians 2:16

2 Corinthians 4:16

2 Corinthians 10:3-6

2 Corinthians 11:3-4

2 Corinthians 11:13-14

Galatians 5:13-26

Galatians 5:16-17

Philippians 4:8

Colossians 1:27

2 Timothy 4:3-5

James 4:7

1 Peter 1:6-7

1 Peter 4:17

1 John 2:15-17

Jude 1:7

Revelations 21:8

Thought Watchers

3 ANGELS & DEMONS

Are you turning the battle to the gate? Are your everyday thoughts conflicting with God's Word? When conflict arises in your life, do you think on the things of God?

Today, war is controversial. Whether civil conflict or national liberation, the effects of war on a nation can be altering. Every gun that is made, every warship launched, every rocket fired signifies conflict and reform. The intensity of battle can ignite aggression, separation, conquest, or in the best of circumstances, unity, peace and positive change. War is an important component of society. This engagement peaks some of the most groundbreaking and pivotal moments in history. In addition to <u>visible</u> confrontations which occur across the world, there are also 'spiritual battles' which embark in the <u>invisible</u> daily.

We have all heard of the phrase, 'the mind is a battlefield.' 'Spiritual Warfare' is the concept of fighting against the work of malevolent forces. It is the Biblical belief regarding evil spirits or demons that are said to intervene in human affairs in various ways. Everything that occurs in the <u>physical world</u> is directly connected to the wrestling match raging in the <u>spiritual world</u>. The enemy operates by deception. He seeks to manipulate, deceive and attack you by tampering with your perception. He seeks to manipulate the truth about God and your worth in Him, starting in your mind.

"Be sober, be vigilant; because your adversary the devil, as a roaring lion, walketh about, seeking whom he may devour," (1 Pet. 5:8). He desires to lead you into sin and disconnect your fellowship with Him. A devoted enemy seeks to wreak havoc on everything that matters to you: your heart, your mind, your marriage, your children, your relationships, your dreams, and your destiny.

This clash of good and evil becomes intense when a person decides to accept Jesus Christ as their Savior. The enemy will use circumstances, events, people, things and even doubt in the mind, to try and steal our heart's back to him. He often attacks us at points of weakness. Wicked temptations show up when we are most vulnerable. Refuse to neglect your soul. Refuse to turn your back to the gospel. Preacher John Bunyan once said, "You can do more than pray - after you have prayed, but you cannot do more than pray - until you have prayed. Pray often, for prayer is a shield to the soul, a sacrifice to God, and a scourge to satan."

Temptation and enticements are not accidental. These deceptive tactics are specifically designed, timed and personalized in hopes that you fall prey to the ploy. Stand firm in your belief. Stay away from satanic witchcraft, horoscopes and psychic phenomenon which can cause great harm to those who get involved. Stay out of sin, fear and unbelief. Christian living is not passive. "Beloved, think it not strange concerning the fiery trial, which is to try you, as though some strange things happened unto you," (1 Pet. 4:12). Just as the agents of God exist, so do the agents of satan.

For centuries, artists have portrayed angels as beautiful humans with wings and glowing light, complete with halos, harps and white flowing gowns. Religion often depicts angels as benevolent celestial beings who act as intermediaries between God (Heaven) and humanity. Their role includes protecting and guiding human beings, and carrying out tasks on behalf of God. Angels serve and protect whichever person God assigns them to and present prayer to God on that person's behalf. Unlike God, who is omnipresent, angels are finite creatures, limited to one place at a time.

The spiritual world has structure, order and levels. For instance, at the high level we have seraphim, cherubim, and thrones. At the middle level is dominions, virtues and powers. At the low level, there are principalities, archangels and angels. An archangel is an angel of the highest rank; in a leadership position. The seven angels of God include: Michael, Gabriel, Raphael, Uriel, Simiel, Oriphiel and Raguel. Daniel is the first Biblical figure to refer to individual angels by name. "For by Him were all things created, that are in Heaven, and that are in Earth, visible and invisible, whether they be thrones, or dominions, or principalities, or powers: all things were created by Him, and for Him..." (Col. 1:16). Angels are powerful and impact the world around us. Their influence often goes unnoticed. All things have been created by Him and for Him.

- "But ye are come unto mount sion, and unto the city of the living God, the Heavenly Jerusalem, and to an innumerable company of angels," (Heb. 12:22).
- "The chariots of the Gods are twenty thousand, even thousands of angels: the Lord is among them, as in Sinai, in the Holy place," (Psa. 68:17).

Come On Outta Here

Becoming a thought watcher, requires you to acknowledge demons exist, attacks are possible, and then be diligent and purposeful in guarding your mind. Many believe in angels, but attest demons to superstitious belief and practice of the ancient world. Nevertheless, over and over scripture depicts these entities as real. Demons are fallen angels who joined satan in his rebellion against God. Satan and his followers were heavenly beings created for good, but of their own free will chose to reject God and become evil. Satan rebelled against God because of his own pride and was cast out of Heaven. "And there was a great war in Heaven: Michael and his

36

angels fought against the dragon; and the dragon fought and his angels, and prevailed not; neither was their place found any more in Heaven, And the great dragon was cast out, that old serpent, called the Devil, and Satan, which decieveth the whole world: he was cast out into the Earth and his angels were cast out with him," (Rev. 12:7-9).

For example, in Luke chapter four, we see Jesus actually possess authority over demonic forces. "Now when the sun was setting, all they had any sick with divers diseases brought them unto Him and He laid hands on every one of them, and healed them. And devils also came out of many, crying out, and saying, Thou art Christ the Son of God. And He rebuking them suffered them not to speak: for they knew that He was Christ," (Lk. 4:40-41). Demons continue to serve the devil in his attempt to lead the world away from God, and into sin. They do this by blinding the mind of unbelievers, so they cannot see the light of the gospel. Also, by promoting false doctrine and introducing seducing spirits. Yet, at the command of Jesus, He rebuked them, suffered them not to speak, and they obeyed.

Demonic possession is a controversial topic today. In various scriptures, we can see how demonic influence caused physical ailments such as an inability to speak, epileptic symptoms, blindness, and the like. In times past, these physical impairments could not be attributed to an actual physiological problem, but rather possession.

♦ "Then was brought unto Him one possessed with a devil, blind, and dumb: and He healed him, insomuch that the blind and dumb both spake and saw. And all the people were amazed, and said, Is not this the son of David?" (Matt. 12:22-23).

♦ "And they were all amazed, insomuch that they questioned among themselves, saying, what things is this? What new doctrine is this? For with authority commandeth He even the unclean spirits, and they do obey Him," (Mk. 1:27).

♦ "(2) And when he was come out of the ship, immediately there met him out of the tombs a man with an unclean spirit, (3)...and no man could bind him with chains (4)...neither could any man tame him. (5) And always, night and day, he was in the mountains, and in the tombs, crying, and cutting himself with stones. (7) And cried with a loud voice, and said, what have I to do with thee, Jesus, thou Son of the most high God? I adjure thee by God, that thou torment me not. (8) For He said unto him, Come out of the man, thou unclean spirit. (9) And He asked him, what is thy name? And he answered, saying, My name is Legion: for we are many," (Mk. 5:1-20).

♦ "Then entered satan into Judas surnamed Iscariot, being of the number twelve," (Lk. 22:3).

♦ "Jesus answered them, Have not I chosen you twelve, and one of you is a devil?" (Jn. 6:70).

- "(43) when the unclean spirit is gone out of a man, he walketh through dry places, seeking rest, and findeth none. (44) Then he saith, I will return into my house from whence I came out, he findeth it empty, swept and garnished. (45) Then goeth he, and taketh with himself seven other spirits more wicked than himself, and they enter in and dwell there: and the last state of that man is worse than the first. Even so shall it be also unto this wicked generation," (Matt. 12:43-45)

The good news is that if we are pursuing God, if we are clothing ourselves with His armor and relying upon His strength, we have nothing to fear. The good news is that if we are watching our thoughts, we have control over these forces. Demons days are numbered. These wicked creatures have an eternal fire prepared and will be bound to an eternity in Hell. We can rest in Heavenly peace, protection and provision knowing that God rules over all!

Are you dressed for the occasion? Buckle the belt of truth around your waist. Cover your heart with the breastplate of righteousness. Protect your feet with the shoes of the gospel of peace. Use the shield of faith to protect yourself from spiritual attacks. Wear the helmet of salvation to protect your mind. Carry the sword of the spirit (the Word of God) to ward off evil.

The "Armor of God" is used to describe a believer's spiritual inventory. If you find yourself struggling with difficult circumstances and unusual feelings of discouragement, it could be a sign that you're facing a spiritual attack. Get dressed! If you find yourself weary and frustrated in your purpose. Get dressed! If you find yourself tempted above what you can handle, at every turn, with no help in sight. Get dressed! These metal pieces described in Ephesians, solid and substantial, are necessary for battle.

The effects of the war going on in the spiritual world, reveal themselves in our minds, our damaged and stained relationships, our emotional instability, mental fatigue and physical exhaustion. The weapons of are warfare are not carnal, but mighty through God to pull down strongholds in our lives. **Our biggest 'natural problems' are a direct representation of a spiritually-rooted dilemma.** The primary nemesis behind anger, unforgiveness, pride, insecurity, discord and fear; are the devil by satanic attack. You shall know the truth and the truth shall make you free. Just because we cannot see the spiritual realm, does not mean it is not operating around us.

Only God allows us to claim victory over evil. Even Jesus was tempted in the wilderness when He fasted forty days and forty nights. "And saith unto him, If thou be the Son of God, cast thyself down: for it is written, He shall give His angels charge concerning thee: and in their hands they shall bear thee up, lest at any time thou dash thy foot against a stone," (Matt 4:1-11).

God's weaponry and defensive instruments are unique. The Israelites walked around the wall of Jericho for seven days carrying the ark of the covenant. On the seventh day, Joshua commanded his people to blow their trumpets made of rams' horns and shout at the walls until they finally fell down. Whether it was King Jehoshaphat singing praise or David using his slingshot to kill Goliath. Whether it was pointy arrows or weapons of prayer. Whether it is guarding the gates of your mind or watching your thoughts. Remember, the Word of God is the only weapon for battle. It is quick and powerful and sharper than any two-edged sword (Heb. 4:12). We must put the Word into our minds, then let those thoughts create Godly action.

"Let the saints be joyful in glory: let them sing aloud upon their beds. Let the high praises of God be in their mouth, and a two edged sword in their hand; to execute vengeance upon the heathen, and punishments upon the people; to bind their kings with chains, and their nobles with fetters of iron; to execute upon them the judgment written: this honour have all His saints. Praise ye the LORD," (Psa. 149:5-9).

The invisible controls the visible. God has provided us with everything we need to win the spiritual encounters we face. Battles will take place whether we are passive or active in engaging in them. We are either victims or victors. Prayer is the divinely authorized mechanism God has given us, to tap into His power. Without it we will be ineffective in spiritual warfare. **Prayer will make a man cease**

41

from sin, or sin will entice a man to cease from prayer. The truths that we know best are learned on our knees. We never know a thing well until it is burned into our hearts by prayer.

Your prayer needs to be authentic and heartfelt. Prayer is how we see Heaven invade Earth. It's what opens the floodgates for God to come down and get involved in our everyday circumstances. "No weapon that is formed against thee shall prosper; and every tongue that shall rise against thee in judgment thou shalt condemn..." (Isa. 54:17). Jesus has come and conquered. The war is already won in the Heavenly realm, but you must actively pray and fight back using the Word of God.

We need to have spiritual vision to understand who we are in Christ. To possess spiritual vision, we should ask the Lord to open our eyes to see the enemy's activity. Guard the gate of your ears and ask God to heighten your spiritual senses. "(18) The eyes of your understanding being enlightened; that ye may know what is the hope of His calling, and what the riches of the glory of His inheritance in the saints, (19) and what is the exceeding greatness of His power to us-ward who believe, according to the working of His mighty power... (21) far above all principality, and power, and might, and dominion, and every name that is named, not only in this world, but also in that which is to come: (22) and hath put all things under His feet... " (Eph. 1:18-23). To defeat and disarm him, we must be more aware of the spiritual resources given to us. We need to know, believe, and act upon the truth. The eyes of the Lord are in every place observing the good and the evil (Prov. 15:3).

A popular adage of Murphy's law states, "Whatever can go wrong, will go wrong." When things go wrong in your life, observe whether these trials were created by God or satan. Created conflicts are necessary to build us up; creating spiritual stamina to prepare us for the 'real fight' with demonic forces. In Isaiah chapter 45 verse 7, it reads, "I form the light, and create darkness: I make peace, and create evil: I the LORD do all these things."

The Suffering of Job

Is Christianity about fighting and suffering or about love and joy?
Isn't Christian living about peace?
Why do I have to suffer if I obey the truth?
Didn't Jesus *do it all* so I would not have to?

These statements have crossed the mind of every believer at some point. In the parable of Job, we explore God's relationship and interaction with human suffering. Job, a wealthy man, is mindful to live in a righteous manner. God brags to satan about Job's virtue, but satan contends that Job is only righteous because God has favored him generously. Satan dares God that, if given approval to inflict suffering, Job will change and curse God. "And the LORD said unto satan, Hast thou considered my servant Job, that there is none like him in the Earth, a perfect and upright man, one that feareth God, and escheweth evil?" (Job 1:8). God permits satan to tempt Job, but He forbids satan to take his life.

Over time, Job's sheep, servants, and ten children have all died due to thieving intruders or natural disasters. Job accuses God of being unjust and not operating the world according to the principles of justice. In his pain, he rips his clothes and shaves his head in sorrow. He still praises God, praying and trying to endure his affliction. Eventually, he turns bitter, anxious, and scared as the suffering becomes too much for him to handle. He deplores injustice; that God lets evil people thrive while he and many other honest people suffer. He wants to face God in protest but cannot physically find God. So, he is certain that there is a "witness" or "Redeemer" in Heaven who will testify for his integrity. "Thou He slay me, yet will I trust Him: but I will maintain mine own ways before Him," (Job 13:15).

God eventually intervenes, commanding Job to be brave. He restores his health, granting him twice as much property as before, new children, and remarkably long life. While we do not always know why we suffer, we can bring our pain and grief to God and trust in His wisdom. "But the God of all grace, who hath called us unto His eternal glory by Christ Jesus, after that ye have suffered a while, make you perfect, stablish, strengthen, settle you," (1 Pet. 5:10). **Being a**

thought watcher will not prevent your suffering, it will prepare you with the strength you need to endure. No man, without trials and temptations, can attain a true understanding of the Holy scriptures. In times of affliction, we are commonly met with the sweetest experiences of God's love. In the end, Job never completely gave up hope or faith in the Lord.

The Good Soldier

The Bible often compares faith-filled living to war. As followers of God, we are commanded to fight the good fight of faith (1 Tim. 6:12). Just as a soldier must train mentally and physically for war, God prepares us for battle before sending us into the trenches. Thought watchers overcome the battle of the mind by using the weapon of the Word, and walking in the spirit.

A soldier who serves in the army is trained by the armed forces. These persons must demonstrate acts of self-sacrifice in the most harrowing circumstances. A soldier can shoot an enemy, dig defensive trenches, and defend their country from attack. The qualities of a 'good soldier' include honesty, courage, self-control, decency, and conviction of purpose.

A good soldier must be single-minded. Not only doing the minimum duty, but one who serves with everything within him. Thank God for the men and women who paid the ultimate price defending our freedom. We must remember them and honor them. We, too, must fight the good fight by enduring hardship, avoiding sin and pleasing the Lord Jesus. "Thou therefore endure hardness, as a good soldier of Jesus Christ. No man that warreth entangleth himself with the affairs of this life; that he may please Him who hath chosen him to be a soldier," (2 Tim. 2:3-4).

There are different levels of skill required to be a soldier. A warrior is an experienced soldier, who specializes in combat. Jesus also endured great hardship. He is the perfect Commander who leads by example and will bring you to certain victory in the end. "(39) See not that I, even I, am He, and there is no God with me: I kill, and I make alive; I wound, and I heal: neither is there any that can deliver out of my hand," (Deut. 32:39).

God is the ultimate warrior. You may not have shed your blood for the faith, nevertheless you will experience hardship as a believer for your faithfulness – *count on it.*

The entire Roman cohort attacked Jesus. They spit on Him. They beat Him. A Roman Soldier often served for twenty years and shockingly these men were not allowed to marry. However, Jesus had prepared himself for what was to come. Preparation for life's battle does not come from only reading the Bible, but from enduring various tests and challenges. Through experiencing spiritual warfare first-hand, a believer's faith, prayer-life, and trust in the Lord will increase. Through experiencing spiritual warfare up close, we can become more aware of incorrect thinking which seeks to enter the gates of our mind. "Behold, I have given unto you power to tread on serpents and scorpions, and over all the power of the enemy: and nothing shall by any means hurt you," (Lk. 10:19). Victory is available to us when we pray for God's help in battle. Victory is a result of right thinking, also positive confession, habits, values, and actions.

The source of true power and strength is spiritual. The Lord has given us His Spirit to empower us to overcome. We must be willing to allow Him the authority to be in control of our emotions, mind, and behaviors. We must operate in the world as a true follower of Christ, not naïve or in ignorance, but having a responsibility to obey the Lord's directions for us at all costs. We are sent into the world to be a "witness" of Jesus Christ. This miraculous calling given to all of us, takes the miracle of the Holy Spirit living in us to fulfill it.

Sealed

The Holy Spirit is a helper. It is a record or 'witness' inside each of us, that we belong to God. Just as a piece of candy is sealed with a wrapper before consumption, we are sealed by the Almighty God. "Who hath also sealed us and given the earnest of the Spirit in our hearts," (2 Cor. 1:22). This Spirit is Christ in you, the hope of glory. Use what God has given you to overcome every difficulty in your life.

This cooling water will give you supernatural strength. God has given you power to make the impossible possible.

This comforter inside of us speaks. During spiritual warfare, this is the only language the devil cannot interpret. The Holy Ghost is an Angel's Tongue given to those who obey Him. You must build yourself up by praying in the Holy Ghost. "He that believeth on me, as the scripture hath said, out of his belly shall flow rivers of living water," (Jn. 7:38). Stay on your knees and pray until help comes. Cry 'Abba Father' until God moves. The Holy Ghost will help you to cast down evil imaginations of the mind. These groanings which cannot be uttered make intercession for us, according to the will of God (Rom. 8:26). "Ye stiffnecked and uncircumcised in heart and ears, ye do always resist the Holy Ghost: as your fathers did, so do ye," (Acts 7:51).

Direct communication to the throne of God comes by speaking, using the Holy Ghost. We must pray in season and out of season. Pray and do not faint or get weary during trouble (Lk. 18:1). Ordained strength comes from our enemies. When we put on the whole armor of God that lifeforce helps our infirmities. We are a special people and God has crowned us with glory and honor. He has made us a little lower than the angels. He has given us dominion over the works of our hands. God has put all things under our feet (Psa. 8:2-6). We must actively live on purpose using this power.

In a real estate transaction, an earnest payment is a security deposit showing good faith about wanting to complete a transaction. Possessing God's Holy language and having the Holy Spirit is your earnest deposit to Heaven. This guarantee of redemption is our proof of salvation before leaving Earth. This is the witness or sign that He lives in you. Don't grieve the Holy Spirit! This presence is our soul's everlasting advocate. Think God and thank God! Know that you are more than a conqueror. The battle does not belong to us, it belongs to Him. "He that believeth on the Son of God hath the witness in himself: he that believeth not God hath made Him a liar; because he believeth not the record that God gave of His Son," (1 Jn. 5:10).

"Holy Spirit Scriptures"

- "When they heard these things, they were cut to the heart, and they gnashed on him with their teeth. But he, being full of the Holy Ghost, looked up stedfastly into Heaven, and saw the glory of God, and Jesus standing on the right hand of God," (Acts 7:54-55).
- "But they were afraid and affrighted, and supposed that they had seen a spirit," (Lk. 24:37).
- "And we are His witnesses of these things; and so is also the Holy Ghost, whom God hath given to them that obey Him," (Acts 5:32)

- "Then Peter said unto them, Repent, and be baptized every one of you in the name of Jesus Christ for the remission of sins, and ye shall receive the gift of the Holy Ghost," (Acts 2:38).

- "But ye shall receive power, after that the Holy Ghost is come upon you: and ye shall be witnesses unto me both in Jerusalem, and in Judaea, and in Samaria, and unto the uttermost part of the Earth," (Acts 1:8).

- "But ye, beloved, building up yourselves on your most Holy faith, praying in the Holy Ghost," (Jude 1:20).

The rivalry of good and evil can also be compared to a football game on Super Sunday. In American football, the offense is the side in which the players have possession of the ball. Their job is to advance the ball towards the opponents end zone to score points. Contrarily, the defensive team is not in possession of the ball and must prevent the other team from scoring. As believers, we must possess a defensive strategy against demonic persuasion and sin. Our offensive strategy is to delight in God, keep His commandments, give, pray, and praise. The best defense is a strong offense. You need both to win. It's gameday! The field is set, the enemy is at your heels, seeking to tackle you and stop your progress. You must keep moving! Resist him, maneuver around his tactics. To achieve your goals, you must press towards the mark which is the high calling of God (Phil. 3:14).

To defend ourselves in the power of God's strength, we must discern where the attacks are likely coming from. **Satan is not clever, just cunning.** Author Sun Tzu is quoted saying, "Know thyself, know thy enemy. A thousand battles, a thousand victories." The Lord protects and provides for us through His angels, as He chooses. "But to which of the angels said He at any time, sit on my right hand until I make thine enemies thy footstool? Are they not all ministering spirits, sent forth to minister for them who shall be heirs of salvation?" (Heb. 1:13-14).

God is a 'pursuing' God who will follow you with goodness and mercy throughout your entire life. *Angel Mercy* and *Angel Goodness* are after you. These guardian angels are purposed to be with you. *Mercy* is defined as a love that responds to human need in an unexpected or unmerited way. At its core, mercy is forgiveness. God's character exemplifies this goodness. It's not just what He does; it's who He is – and who He is never changes. He is our refuge and strength. A present help in times of trouble. Psalm 23 discusses God's protection through the Valley of Death. His presence implies protection; this is a promise. "Surely goodness and mercy shall follow me all the days of my life: and I will dwell in the House of the Lord for ever," (Psa. 23:6).

The best of believers are often found in the worst of times. Be kind to everyone you meet. Charity is the highest form of love. Altruism or 'do-gooding' is the ultimate perfection of the human spirit, both glorifying and reflecting the nature of God. Angels are all around us. "The Lord hath prepared His throne in the Heavens; and His Kingdom ruleth over all. Bless the Lord, ye His angels, that excel in strength, that do His commandments, hearkening unto the voice of His Word," (Psa. 103:19-20). You never know the personal battle an individual may be going through. John Bunyan's famous quote says, "You have not lived today until you have done something for someone who can never repay you."

The Bible commands us to love others above all things. Be careful of having a lifestyle that does not match your words. The writer Paul says people like this are empty, shallow, sharp, banging noises that eventually become an irritant to all who hear them. "Though I speak with the tongues of men and of angels, and have not charity, I am become as sounding brass, or a tinkling cymbal," (1 Cor. 13:1).

Be forgiving and tenderhearted. Let the love of God shine through you everywhere you go. At the stoplight, give what you can to the homeless man. In the grocery store, help the elderly woman needing assistance. On your job, give a kind word to your neighbor who is going through. Stand with those facing persecution. Show hospitality to ministers from other countries. "Be not forgetful to entertain strangers: for thereby some have entertained angels unawares," (Heb. 13:2).

Have you ever talked to an angel without knowing it? The context of this passage in Hebrews 13, is not describing meetings with Heavenly messengers. It refers to showing special attention or hospitality to those traveling or in need. To express brotherly love. Hospitality gives you the privilege of blessing others. Cultivating a lifestyle that regards other people brings happiness.

My Chapter Notes:

_____

_____

_____

_____

_____

Reference Scriptures:

Deuteronomy 32:39

Job 1:8

Job 13:15

Psalm 8:2-6

Psalm 23:6

Psalm 68:17

Psalm 149:5-9

Psalm 103:19-20

Proverbs 15:3

Isaiah 45:7

Isaiah 54:17

Matthew 4:1-11

Matthew 12:22-23

Matthew 12:43-45

Mark 1:27

Mark 5:1-20

Luke 4:40-41

Luke 10:19

Luke 18:1

Luke 22:3

Luke 24:37

John 6:70

John 7:38

Acts 1:8

Acts 2:38

Acts 5:32

Acts 7:51, 54-55

Romans 8:26

1 Corinthians 13:1

2 Corinthians 1:22

Ephesians 1:18-23

Philippians 3:14

Colossians 1:16

1 Timothy 6:12

2 Timothy 2:3-4

Hebrews 1:13-14

Hebrews 4:12

Hebrews 12:22

Hebrews 13:2

1 Peter 4:12

1 Peter 5:8, 10

1 John 5:10

Jude 1:20

Revelations 12:7-9

4 THE FIRE OF GOD

In numerous examples throughout Scripture, also as seen in previous chapters, we how this unseen battle between the flesh and the spirit has been waged throughout history and today. As believers in the faith, we each suffer various afflictions and are tempted in different ways. Fire can be seen all throughout the Word of God. Throughout Scripture, the presence of God physically manifests as fire, and is needed to cast down strongholds, to set us free from our flesh, to keep our minds stayed on Him, and subdue the enemy in our lives.

Both mesmerizing and mysterious, *fire* has intrigued minds since the early days of humanity. Whether it's the red-hot glow against a midnight sky or the auburn tango of the flame in the wind, it has always been a constant source of interest and debate. Discovered millions of years ago, when it lingered and struck fear in the hearts of cavemen, fire can now be explained scientifically as a process of chemical combustion that releases both heat and light. **Thought**

watchers embrace the fire of God as a much needed tool to cleanse the mind and the spirit.

Today, we think of the concept 'fire' practically as a use for cooking, igniting a candle for light, or striking a match for warmth. Yet, the *spiritual fire* as seen in the Bible metaphorically represents an instrument of warfare, sanctification, and purification. Of great importance, the word "fire" itself is mentioned over 500 times in the King James Version of the Bible. "Is not my Word like as a fire? saith the Lord; and like a hammer that breaketh the rock in pieces?" (Jer. 23:29).

In understanding the flesh and the spirit, it is important to understand how God uses this inferno in our lives to develop and give strength to the inner-man. "Wherein ye greatly rejoice, though now for a season, if need be, ye are in heaviness through manifold temptations: that the trial of your faith, being much more precious than of gold that perisheth, though it be tried with fire, might be found unto praise and honour and glory at the appearing of Jesus Christ," (1 Pet. 1:6-7). The text, *'If need be,'* literally means if God thinks we need the affliction. If He, in His eternal wisdom, sees it as necessary that we go through this trial or that hardship to become a better version of ourselves.

Think of your weaknesses and your struggles? You will often find that your 'manifold temptations' are linked to areas in your life that you are weak in your inner-man, or 'fleshly' characteristics God is trying to prune away from us. "For our God is a consuming fire," (Heb. 12:29). If you are walking in your flesh, you are a slave to sin. A slave to cigarettes, lying, backbiting, cursing, adultery, or fornication. This means inevitably that the dangerous desire you are struggling with is holding you captive and remember there is no middle ground to Heaven (Josh. 24:15). Thought watchers become more and more aware of strategies of sin, and as a result can prevent them from happening. **Stop sin before it starts, starting in the mind.** This can only be accomplished with God's help and through His Word. The fire of God manifests in our lives to release us and to set us free from what has us bound.

Freedom from the flesh is found in God's Word. Freedom from the flesh is felt in the fire. This righteous blaze from Heaven demonstrates God's anger and righteous judgment over humanity. "I form the light, and create darkness: I make peace, and create evil: I the LORD do all these things," (Isa. 45:7). Evil, disorder, temptation, havoc, and chaos are created by God. He is testing you. He is testing the world. "In flaming fire taking vengeance on them that know not God, and that obey not the gospel of our Lord Jesus Christ," (2 Thess. 1:8).

Being purified by the fire is not pretty, or cool, or a "liked" undertaking. Circumstances can seem grueling when God is delivering you from the flesh. Stay encouraged and glorify God in His wisdom for making our souls brand new. "(13) Every man's work shall be made manifest: for the day shall declare it, because it shall be revealed by fire; and the fire shall try every man's work of what sort it is... (15) If any man's work shall be burnt, he shall suffer loss: but he himself shall be saved; yet so as by fire," (1 Cor. 3:13, 15). Only those ordained for Heaven can believe. You cannot win this war on your own. Allow God to step in and work. The affliction, the trials, and the heat are helping to mold you.

The pressures of this world, the heaviness of affliction, the chaos and disarray are needed to manifest who you really are. Known as the 'Philosopher of Happiness,' author Jonathan Lockwood Huie is quoted saying, "The cleansing fire of the spirit consumes the troubles of this world. Feed your concerns to the fire. Breathe deeply and rejoice." If you know that something you are doing is unacceptable in the eyes of God and you have no remorse, no desire to get it out, and no inspiration to stop, you will not escape damnation or the grips of Hell. When your outer-man does wrong, Ask yourself: Do I feel bad? Do I want to do that again? **Do my thoughts accuse me or *excuse* me?** (Rom. 2:15).

Being in the fire cleanses you, it makes you strong and sanctifies you. In addition to sanctification, fire also represents His power, Holiness, and protection over His people. The inner-man must be strengthened in order to conquer the flesh. The flesh doesn't ever really 'go away,' your desires and carnality will always be 'with you.' However, through the supernatural power of God you CAN control your actions. Through His Word, we have the ability to seek His face and turn aside from wickedness. "And then shall the wicked be revealed, whom the Lord shall consume with the spirit of His mouth, and shall destroy with the brightness of His coming," (2 Thess. 2:8).

Your inner-man must love the TRUTH. You are of a righteous seed and cannot regard your past iniquities, get rid of any hidden sins. "If I regard iniquity in my heart, the Lord will not hear me," (Psa. 66:18). Seek wise-counsel when your spirit is unsure of what to do. Developing the inner-man requires us to have a deeper relationship with God. "Who maketh His angels spirits; His ministers a flaming fire," (Psa. 104:4).

A little bit of light pushes a lot of darkness away. Don't fear the fire. Step into the righteous flames of self-discovery. Step into the role of a thought watcher who is consciously aware of right and wrong influences. *Remember, the fire will not burn you; it will only burn what you are not.* If you've ever fallen down and lost your spark, get back up again. You are the son of God. You are the daughter of a King. "The same boiling water that softens the potato hardens the egg, it's not about your circumstances it's about what your made of." Ask God to change you from the inside out.

You heart is a battleground! Everyday your heart is being lured away from God by so many things. **Do you feel like you are in a spiritual battle?** The conflict between good and evil is a universal battle that has always existed and continues today. The spiritual battle is not just a war between angels and demons, but also a war within you. The flesh and spirit of man are at war with each other. Your thoughts, both good and bad, are at war with each other. "Through faith we understand that the worlds were framed by the Word of God, so that the things which are seen were not made of things which do appear," (Heb. 11:3). We cannot be indifferent towards the thoughts we harbor and accept in our hearts. Our thoughts are revealed in the words that we speak (Matt. 12:34). Allow God to perfect you and purify you on the inside.

It's confusing to think some people are innately good and some people intrinsically bad, however people can display a combination of both good and bad qualities. We should desire to show qualities that reflect the nature of Christ. There is no moment more central in history than Jesus sacrificing Himself on the cross, to save all of humanity. He died so that we can crucify the flesh. He died so we can surrender our sinful nature. There is no pleasure in unrighteousness, but God gives us a choice.

When we tend to see our problems in non-spiritual terms, we tend to seek non-spiritual solutions. It's only the spirit that can overcome the passions and desires of the flesh. The only way to fight the spiritual battle that is taking place inside of us, is to counter-attack those ideas with the Truth. Every thought must obey Christ. Stay encouraged during this process of refining, do not give up in the midst of the fire! The destination of your soul is a battle worth fighting for. Your peace, your future, and your freedom is worth fighting for. Your family, your deliverance, and your inner-man is worth fighting for!

Hold on! **Continue to allow the fire within you to burn brighter than the fire around you.** Allow God to move in your life and your spirit. "And I will bring the third part through the fire, and will refine them as silver is refined, and will try them as gold is tried: they shall call on my name, and I will hear them: I will say, It is my people: and they shall say, The Lord is my God," (Zech. 13:9).

Everything in nature is made up of four basic elements: earth, water, *fire,* and air. The flame is the visible portion of the fire. The color of the flame will be different based on the fire's intensity, depending on the temperature. It needs oxygen, heat, an ignition source, and fuel to burn bright, without it the fire will extinguish.

- ♦ **White Fire:** The area near the ground where most burning is occurring
- ♦ **Yellow Fire:** The hottest color of the fire, burning of organic material
- ♦ **Orange Fire:** Slightly cooler temperature
- ♦ **Red Fire:** The coolest region of the fire
- ♦ **Black Smoke:** The region where combustion no longer occurs

We must be determined to follow Christ despite suffering and heartache. Even Paul references "walking in the flesh," referring to his mortal condition in the world, as a human being with limitations and weaknesses. "And He said to them all, If any man will come after me, let him deny himself, and take up his cross daily, and follow me," (Lk. 9:23).

We often pray against an <u>external enemy</u>; spiritual warfare is mostly against *outside forces*. However, the flesh consists of an *inside force,* an <u>internal enemy</u> as well, *ourselves*. Negative thinking can cause you to be an enemy to yourself. We can speak blessings or curses over our lives, and in the lives of others. We can think unrighteous thoughts and desire ungodly things. Be cautious of the kind of attention you kindle, be mindful of the state of your spirit. "Where no wood is, there the fire goeth out: so where there is no talebearer, the strife ceaseth," (Prov. 26:20).

No physical weapons are suitable or appropriate to engage this enemy, divine power is needed to destroy strongholds. **The Word of God works as a spiritual weapon.** "For the Word of God is quick, and powerful, and sharper than any two-edged sword, piercing even to the dividing asunder of soul and spirit, and of the joints and marrow, and is a discerner of thoughts and intents of the heart," (Heb. 4:12). There is an unseen wrestling match playing out in the spirit realm against the kingdom of light and the kingdom of darkness, eternal life or eternal death. The primary nemesis is the devil, but this battle for control over your flesh and spirit has already been won. We are in this world, but not of it. God desires that we should experience His supernatural power; so pray, fast, worship, praise, and repent. The power of Christ gives us victory and dominion over our outer-man. Be committed to think of God! Watch your thoughts.

Stress is the gap between our expectation and reality. Know your triggers! Be cognizant of what activates your negative actions, thoughts, and impulses. Being unaware or unwilling to take accountability for your thinking and actions, causes more mistakes. *What triggered you to sin? Who hindered you that you did not obey the truth?* Once you become aware, take responsibility, and clean house! In practical terms, this can mean unsubscribing from that naughty station, deleting that phone number, throwing away the drugs, coming to church for spiritual counsel, or reading your Bible more. You can overcome lust and temptation, addiction and sin, through spiritual awareness which can only be done through listening to God's wisdom while in the fire. **Help God, help you!** "But every man is tempted, when he is drawn away of his own lusts, and enticed. Then when lust hath conceived, it bringeth forth sin: and sin, when it is finished, bringeth forth death," (Jam. 1:14-15).

A tiny still voice will say, "You shouldn't have done that.".... "I told you not to go here.".…"Why don't you turn that off?"... "Don't talk to that person, it's a trap." We shouldn't be fearful of what may come through our choices, but we should always be prayerful and on guard against the tactics that the enemy sends to entice and provoke our human nature. The flesh is willing, but the Spirit is weak. *The enemy knows your triggers, flaws, and limitations.... Do you?*

Famous Parables on Fire in the Bible

Fire is used constantly throughout Scripture and is depicted as a metaphor for trials that enter a believer's life; such things purify character in the same way that fire purifies precious metals. Whether fire was represented by a burning bush as seen with Moses in Exodus, or depicted as God's presence by wall of fire to protect the Israelites during their escape, or as scorching rain to purify sin during the judgment of Sodom and Gomorrah, it is a key element used to depict Holiness and sanctification in both positive and undesirable contexts.

"Fourth Man in the Fire "

In Daniel, the third Chapter, Shadrach, Meshach, and Abednego neglected to follow the orders of King Nebuchadnezzar. They failed to bow down and worship an idol, the large golden image of the King as commanded. They were sentenced to be cast into the fiery furnace to die, as punishment for their disobedience. "If it be so, our God whom we serve is able to deliver us from the burning fiery furnace, and He will deliver us out of thine hand, O King," (Dan. 3:17). The King was full of fury and wanted to make an example out of them. They were bound, tied, and cast into the flames.

As they watched, the King was astonished and rose up in a hurry amongst talk from his counsellors, "(24) ...Did not we cast three men bound in the middle of the midst of the fire? They answered and said unto the king, True, O king. (25) He answered and said, Lo, I see four men loose, walking in the midst of the fire, and they have no hurt; and the form of the fourth is like the Son of God," (Dan. 3:24-25). The fire had no power, no hair on their head was singed, there coats were not changed, nor did they even have the stench of ash upon them. The people were convinced this was truly the work of God, no other God can deliver or save in this manner. Instead, the King promoted them because he knew God was with them (Isa. 43:2).

As seen in this representation of the fourth man in the fire, this is a portrayal of God's protection. In Holiness, we need to have this same mindset when the flesh or wicked schemes seek to disadvantage us. Or when we are commanded to follow instructions or obey worldly principles, not of God. Proclaim out loud like the three Hebrew boys **"If it be so."** *If it be so*, you will condemn me for doing what is right. *If it be so*, I will suffer for a righteous cause. *If it be so*, you will throw me in the fire for my belief in God. *If it be so*, you will punish me for maintaining my integrity. *If it be so*, you will take all my goods and all that I have.

"Elijah and the Chariots of Fire"

God used fire as a direct display of His presence and power, in addition to a means of sanctification and judgment. In 2 Kings, the second Chapter, the prophet Elijah defended the true God of Israel from the false gods of Baal in the land. Elisha asked for a double portion of His spirit (again symbolizing the flesh and the Spirit). "And it came to pass, as they still went on, and talked, that behold, there appeared a chariot of fire, and horses of fire, and parted them both asunder; and Elijah went up by a whirlwind into Heaven," (2 Kgs. 2:11).

Elijah is known for bringing fire down from Heaven in this regard. This battle over the flesh and the spirit can also be seen in this example, as Elijah was determined to proclaim the Truth and acknowledge the one true God.

"Fire and Brimstone"

In the Bible, fire and brimstone are used to express God's wrath. In Sodom and Gomorrah, in Genesis 19, this is a widely known example of destruction by fire, as representation of God's wrath. He overthrew the inhabitants because of their excessive sin and the country went up as the smoke of a furnace. Again, the flesh was devoured when God's spirit was kindled.

- ♦ "Upon the wicked he shall rain snares, fire and brimstone, and a horrible tempest: this shall be the portion of their cup," (Psa. 11:6).
- ♦ "Then the Lord rained upon Sodom and upon Gomorrah brimstone and fire from the Lord out of Heaven," (Gen. 19:24).

Thankfully, we now have access to an intercessor for our Salvation, through Jesus. We can repent of our sins and choose another way, Christ saving us from our own destruction.

"The Burning Bush"

Can you imagine being alone and something moves behind you? How about God setting a tree on fire and you hearing His voice from the flames? Well, in Exodus Chapter 2-3, we see Moses is visited by God and again experiences a representation of fire, as His presence. "And the angel of the Lord appeared unto him in a flame of fire out of the midst of a bush: and he looked, and behold, the bush burned with fire, and the bush was not consumed," (Exod. 3:2). In this passage, God gives Moses instruction on how to bring the people out of the captivity of Egypt.

* * *

Over and over, we witness the flesh and the spirit combatting throughout Scripture. It important to recognize God's intent to use whatever means necessary to help deliver His children. Whether through love, by the dying of His son on the cross, or by means of fire through sanctification. Unfortunately, everyone in the body of believers will not make it to Heaven. It should be our earnest desire, to separate ourselves from anything that is not like God. In the store, in schools, and in the church, there will be children of the flesh and children of the spirit. "For there must be also heresies among you, that they which are approved may be made manifest among you," (1 Cor. 11:19).

Who are you? Who do you belong to? Hear my words and listen to understand today. I pray that your eyes be enlightened and that you see to understand, and that you hear to make changes. I pray that you think a new thought, and that revelation is sparked in your mind. "He answered and said unto them, Because it is given to you to know the mysteries of the kingdom of Heaven, but to them it is not given," (Matt. 13:11).

God is a loving God, but He is also the most righteous judge that I know. Hell is a real place. This Earth is just a holding ground for the day of judgment. Listen to the Spirit of God, it will often give warning in a still small voice, or contrarily in an intense smoldering indication. Heed the voice of wise-counsel and stay on the straight and narrow path. Draw closer to God and walk in His steps. In doing these things, you are one step closer to making Heaven.

My Chapter Notes:

_____

_____

_____

_____

_____

_____

Thought Watchers

Reference Scriptures:

Genesis 19:24

Exodus 3:2

Joshua 24:15

2 Kings 2:11

Psalm 11:6

Psalm 66:18

Psalm 104:4

Proverbs 26:20

Isaiah 43:2

Isaiah 45:7

Jeremiah 23:29

Daniel 3:17

Daniel 3:24-25

Zechariah 13:9

Matthew 12:34

Matthew 13:11

Luke 9:23

Romans 2:15

1 Corinthians 3:13, 15

1 Corinthians 11:19

2 Thessalonians 1:8

2 Thessalonians 2:8

Hebrews 4:12

Hebrews 11:3

Hebrews 12:29

James 1:14-15

1 Peter 1:6-7

5 THOUGHT WATCHERS

Imagine being in an important meeting at work. You are well-put together, your work material was turned in on time, your coffee is hot, you got the good parking spot, and you're feeling good as you look forward to a productive day. Then, suddenly, your 'known to be challenging' boss or supervisor stops speaking, turns to you in upset, and begins to reprimand you at maximum volume for your recent actions. His hands are flailing in every direction, his face flushed red, and the room is still. Talk about presentation downer! In that moment, your world starts to crash. Everything seems to be moving in slow motion as you digest what is happening around you. Your competitive co-worker Sue is snickering. Bob puts his head down and taps his pen in discomfort. Your trainee, Jill, is shaking her head in disappointment. Your coffee got cold too.

Right away, every impulsive thought that crosses your mind is being broadcast on a screen behind you, for your fellow associates, executives, and manager to now see your wayward feelings.

"Oh, great! Right now?" you silently think to yourself. *"How do I turn this live airing of my mind off?"*

Nope.

Open it back up.

Turn the fictional screen back on.

We want to <u>watch</u> what you are thinking.

Ask yourself, "Do my thoughts represent the flesh or the spirit?" We can chuckle when envisioning this imagined situation, which seems all too real. Yet, it remains true that when recalling a positive memory, a negative decision, or a reflective thought in the privacy of our own minds, we are talking to ourselves all of the time. A teenager who gets grounded for missing curfew. A parent who is called down to the principal's office for their child fighting. The individual who just got a larger than expected bill. In all of these scenarios and various others, we can almost visualize what someone else might be thinking in their frustration. "And the Spirit of the LORD fell upon me, and said unto me, Speak; Thus saith the LORD; Thus have ye said, O House of Israel: for I know the things that come into your mind, every one of them," (Ezek. 11:5).

When upset, our thoughts being displayed for others to see publicly and "live-in-color," is not ideal. Daily, we unconsciously complain about other people and have negative chit-chat with ourselves in our minds. Subconsciously, moderating our own lives with silent sub-titles. Have you ever asked yourself, "Why did I say that?" after a sarcastic outburst. Or encouraged yourself thinking, "You've got it! You can do this," when taking on a difficult task.

Private or public, our thoughts are free to go anywhere, but for many individuals it is surprising how often they head in a negative direction. American philosopher and psychologist, William James is quoted saying, "A great many people think they are thinking when they are merely rearranging their prejudices." For some, viewing your private perspective and thoughts would be a comedic commentary, for others a source of shock, and then regret.

The good news is that through the Word of God, we have the power to control what we think. *Thoughts* play a beneficial role when planning, organizing, and coming up with new ideas. **Thoughts originate from the outside *and* the inside. Ultimately, what we let into our mind shapes the state of our souls.** Our world, our life, and our reality is shaped by our perception and thinking, we become what we think. "For as [a man] thinketh in his heart, so is he..." (Prov. 23:7).

We should always be cautious of the thoughts that enter our ear gate and cross our minds. As you reflect, consider elevating your thoughts. **If you're *thinking already*, you might as well think big.** With each day comes new strength and new thoughts. Your mindset matters. Uplift yourself through the Word of God. "Many, O LORD my God, are thy wonderful works which thou hast done, and thy thoughts which are to us-ward: they cannot be reckoned up in order unto thee: if I would declare and speak of them, they are more than can be numbered," (Psa. 40:5).

Every positive thought is a silent prayer. If you realized how powerful your reflections are, you would never think a negative thought again. **The greatest weapon against stress is our ability to choose one thought over another.** Outside thinking comes from the enemy. God's thoughts are always within us, even when we fail to meditate on them and believe. Pray for wisdom to discern the good and the evil. His thoughts are not our thoughts, nor are His ways our ways.

Control each and every imagination. **When your thinking is derailed, there are no survivors. Our thoughts should not be able to move an inch without running into God's Word.** "That ye be not soon shaken in mind or be troubled, neither by Spirit, nor by Word, nor by letter as from us, as that the day of Christ is at hand," (2 Thess. 2:2). Keep your mind off things that don't help you. Business Developer & CEO, Brian Tracy is quoted as saying, "There are no limits to what you can accomplish, except the limits you place on your own thinking."

According to a 2017 article from Soul Analyse with Stephanie Dunleavy, it is estimated that we each encounter around 60,000 thoughts a day. **The problem isn't necessarily related to the quantity of our thoughts, but the quality.** The practice is to focus on those uplifting thoughts, the ones that make us feel good about who we are and where we are going. "Fulfill ye my joy, that ye be likeminded, having the same love, being of one accord, of one mind. Let nothing be done through strife or vainglory; but in lowliness of mind let each esteem other better than themselves," (Phil. 2:2-3).

Fleshly thoughts arise when we do not identify and recognize wrong beliefs. Once you recognize a thought that is not reflective of the mind of Christ, you must cast that imagination down. Throw it out! We must subject any 'high thing' that is contrary to the Word of God hostage, holding it captive and not allowing it to penetrate our inner-man (2 Cor. 10:3-5). Nothing can harm you as much as your own unguarded thinking. Happiness is just a thought away. Hope is just a prayer away. Prosperity is near. Your faith and your praise open the door.

Choose your thoughts carefully. **Keep what brings you peace, release what brings you suffering.** The fruit of ungodly thoughts must be made manifest. "Hear, O Earth, I will bring evil upon this people, even the fruit of their thoughts, because they have not hearkened unto my words, nor to my law, but rejected it," (Jer. 6:19). If constructive and Godly thoughts are planted, positive outcomes will be the result. **Plant positive seeds!** You feed your mind daily by what you read, see, and hear. *Watch what you digest.* Sow good things to the inside, with being cautious about what you intake from the outside. Build your mind muscles and stay encouraged, as you seek to strengthen the inner-man.

Fellow author and Christian Minister, George MacDonald is quoted sharing his beliefs, "If instead of a gem or even a flower we should cast the gift of loving thought into the heart of a friend, that would be giving as the angels give." In certain seasons trees have no fruit, yet in the right season the harvest comes back again. Help us reap souls, by blessing God's House. You can program your mind to meditate on all of His promises, this is a strong tool for growth and positive improvement in your life. Pull up any weeds of wickedness from your brain, and grow in the knowledge and thoughts of God.

Will you step into the role of a thought watcher today? There is always room to become a better person. "Put on therefore, as the elect of God, Holy and beloved, bowels of mercies, kindness, humbleness of mind, meekness, longsuffering; Forbearing one another, and forgiving one another, if any man have a quarrel against any: even as Christ forgave you, so also do ye. And above all these things put on charity, which is the bond of perfectness," (Col. 3:12-14).

To be perfect in Him, we must think like Him. Yes! **Think God!** This phrase, *'Think God'* means to think like God, to think on the things of God, and to be mindful of Him in all that we do. "Let this mind be in you, which was also in Christ Jesus," (Phil. 2:5). Happiness is a state of mind, not something we acquire. There is a difference between our faith-filled experience "in here" and our negative emotions "out there," (Jn. 16:33). God wants to develop our spirit man from the inside-out.

Your mind is the dwelling place of your thoughts. One small positive thought in the morning can transform your whole day. Study to be quiet and mind your own business (1 Thess. 4:11-12). Wash your heart from wickedness. God cannot think evil. He can create evil because of His love for us, to chastise us and draw us closer to Him. However, He does not think evil things, if *you* do – then, your thinking is not aligned with His mind. Out of the heart proceed immoral intentions and fleshly fantasies, which defile the inner-man. "For out of the heart proceed evil thoughts, murders, adulteries, fornications, thefts, false witness, blasphemies..." (Matt. 15:19).

How long shall vain thoughts lodge within you? Watch what you consider and be mindful to reject things that do not glorify God. God hates vain thoughts. *Vain* is defined as being proud of your own appearance, your own achievements, and your own abilities. "I hate vain thoughts: but thy law do I love," (Psa. 119:113). The ego is like dust in the mind, clean away the dust and you see things more clearly.

Vanity, pride, arrogance, and the ego are all undesirable conditions that can plague the mind. These sinful and shallow appreciations of 'the self,' limit your ability to truly develop the inner-man. You must go deeper. Delve deeper in God, deeper into His Word, and explore a deeper understanding of yourself. "Your iniquities have turned away these things, and your sins have withholden good things from you," (Jer. 5:25). When you love the law of God, vain thoughts cannot come into your inner dwelling.

All throughout Scripture, God brought destruction in times of sin and wickedness. "And God saw that the wickedness of man was great in the Earth, and that every imagination of the thoughts of his heart was only evil continually," (Gen. 6:5). Disease, famine, fire, and catastrophes of flood were brought as a way to cleanse the Earth from sin, in times past. As believers today, we are called a part to be Holy, to be different and peculiar amongst others. We are called not to walk after the affections of this world (the Gentiles) and Earthly things, but to be aware and conscious of a higher calling. **We are in the Earth but not of the Earth. We are in the flesh but not of the flesh.** Our minds should operate, and function aligned with God's mind. "(17) This I say therefore, and testify in the Lord, that ye henceforth walk not as other Gentiles walk, in the vanity of their mind, (18) Having their understanding darkened, being alienated from the life of God though the ignorance that is in them, because of the blindness of their heart...(20) But ye have not so learned Christ...(22) That ye put off concerning the former conversation the old man, which is corrupt according to the deceitful lusts; (23) And be renewed in the spirit of your mind," (Eph. 4:17-23).

Make a choice today! Take your mind to Heavenly places, above the mayhem on the Earth. Rise above it all by resting in His Word and laying down the cares of this world at His feet. Hold yourself accountable for what you say, do, and think as you strive to be more like Jesus. Do your best to prepare yourself in this life, for where you may go in the next. **Overcome the flesh and walk in the Spirit of God, by becoming a thought watcher.** "For they that are after the flesh do mind the things of the flesh; but they that are after the Spirit the things of the Spirit. For to be carnally minded is death; but to be spiritually minded is life and peace," (Rom. 8:5-6).

Today, national instability continues to run rampant. During pandemic and pandemonium, God covers His children. Even watching the news, you must guard the gate of your ears and the gate of your mind, be alert of what T.V. broadcast or news bulletin you allow to affect your inner-man. "Whose end is destruction, whose God is in their belly, and whose glory is in their shame, who mind Earthly things. For our conversation is in Heaven; from whence also we look for the Saviour, the Lord Jesus Christ," (Phil. 3:19-20).

Time after time, God sends destruction to get the world's attention. In times like these, He is <u>demanding</u> awareness and serving notice of His return. *Will you hear His voice today?* Coronavirus is not here by accident. All throughout Scripture God sends plagues, destruction and evil, as well as good. Angels have always brought pestilence, outbreaks, affliction and disease in Biblical times and they always comes from, or are allowed by God. If you are suffering in your mind or need healing in your body, stay connected to the true vine -

Jesus. In Him, no plague shall come near our dwelling (Ex. 30:12; Psa. 91:10).

Plan for eternity, you have never seen *tomorrow*. Every time you wake up, *today* shows up all over again. Being in charge of our life requires surrendering to God and commanding our emotions. Peace of mind is about being present and appreciating the here and now. "This I recall to my mind, therefore have I hope," (Lam. 3:21). Your life purpose should define your thoughts, not the other way around. As believers our purpose is towards the Kingdom of God, serving others, building His House and focusing on making it to Heaven. "For behold, I create new Heavens and a new Earth: and the former shall not be remembered, nor come into mind," (Isa. 65:17). Release your past struggles, release the former things that have kept you bound, and press on in God. **Continue to *elevate your thinking,* by watching *what* you are thinking.** Pray in the Holy Ghost, strengthen the inner-man, and stand firm in the faith.

In Holiness, our thoughts should be rooted in the teachings of Jesus. They are founded, developed, and nurtured based on the Word of God. Our whole purpose as believers is striving to live a life, as Christ did. **Having a positive approach is having a Heavenly approach.** Having faith does not mean being overly optimistic or naive, instead it allows us to become the best version of ourselves given our current set of circumstances. "(23) But I see another law in my members, warring against the law of my mind, and bringing me into captivity to the law of sin which is in my members (24) O wretched man that I am!... (25) I thank God through Jesus Christ our Lord. So then with the mind I myself serve the law of God; but with the flesh the law of sin," (Rom. 7:23-25).

Action without thought is impulsiveness, thought without action is procrastination. We all have positive or negative thoughts, and moments. In the faith, we must not ignore reality. Pretending that our flesh is not present and avoiding any negative emotions, will not make them go away. The way to deal with ungodly thoughts doesn't involve trying to stop our thinking itself, doing so would cause us to be vacant, dull, and empty. The solution lies in shifting from being overpowered by our thoughts, to being aware of them from an outside perspective looking in.

Be aware of repetitive thoughts that you experience regularly, and notice the chaos they create without reacting or becoming absorbed in them. Silently observe the thoughts in your head, as if the voice of someone else, watch them as words being spoken. Don't judge these thoughts or battle with them, create peace and dissolve conflict within yourself by meditating on the Word of God.

How to Overcome Ungodly Thoughts:

1 – Watch your Thoughts

2 - Acknowledge the Negative Ideas that you are Thinking

3 – Be Aware of your Response and the Negative Emotions that Attempt to Arise

4 – Meditate on the Word of God regarding your Situation

5 – Act Accordingly to Resolve the Situation

(Always seek wise counsel if needed)

Our words are a manifestation of the thoughts going on in our brains. Words can calm us or excite us. Create intimacy or separation (Mk. 7:20). Increase our power or allow us to live in defeat. However, people often assume that what you don't talk about, you don't think about. This is untrue, we can also think something and constrain ourselves, by choosing to speak life instead of death (Prov. 18:21). A word not spoken is a word not born. Yet, that doesn't mean the thought was not present. "Finally, brethren, whatsoever things are true, whatsoever things are honest, whatsoever things are just, whatsoever things are pure, whatsoever things are lovely, whatsoever things are of a good report; if there be any virtue, and if there be any praise, think on these things," (Phil. 4:8).

Be mindful of your thoughts and consider the internal dialogue of others as well. Remember, outsiders will always have an opinion about you looking in. Their view is not always the full picture. **Don't believe everything you hear. Don't accept everything you think.** Caring about what other people think about you will always keep you as their prisoner. You will never succeed with an inferior mindset, be humble, but know you are in God, be conscious of what the Word says about you. You are more than a conqueror. Close your ears and guard your mind; ignore the naysayers. You should care about what God knows about you and what He thinks of you. Speak your truth, obey God, and follow Him (1 Jn. 2:19).

Thought Affirmation:

Watch your thoughts, they become your words.
Watch your words, they become your actions.
Watch your actions, they become your habits.
Watch your habits, they become values.
Watch your values, it will become your destiny.

Our days are full of small little "habits" that we do unconsciously, whether it be being late or early, messy or tidy, rude or courteous. Our character comes from the thoughts and actions we do habitually over time. Often, when we are harsh, critical, and judgmental, those negative thoughts and actions push others away. *People want to be around people who think positive!* "Unto the pure all things are pure: but unto them that are defiled, and unbelieving is nothing pure; but even their mind and conscience is defiled," (Tit. 1:15). Thus, by holding positive thoughts and habitually taking positive action, God can create good character in us. With a sound mind, you are destined for upliftment and you are destined to succeed.

Becoming aware of our brain-power and the strength of our mind is a process. Effectually, working to categorize our thoughts and then decide what to do with them, also takes practice. **Living a life of faith does not come overnight, but if you commit and become a student of the Word, change will come.** "Among whom also we all had our conversation in times past in the lusts of our flesh, fulfilling the desires of the flesh and the mind; and were by nature the children of wrath, even as others," (Eph. 2:3). With God's help and understanding the brain as discussed in Scripture, we can be better prepared to handle 'mind matters' in our lives.

A person's attitude or mental state is referred to as their *mindset*. This mental characteristic will often determine how you will interpret and respond to situations. It also involves your beliefs, feelings, values, and disposition to act in certain ways. In the flesh, we operate in a carnal mindset, paralleling our lives and decisions to worldly figures, the media and trends. In the Spirit of God, believers operate based on the Bible, following the teachings and actions of Jesus, as well as leadership on how we should deal with decisions in our lives. "For this is the covenant that I will make with the House of Israel after those days, saith the Lord; I will put my laws into their mind, and write them in their hearts, and I will be to them a God, and they shall be to me a people," (Heb. 8:10).

Think about it. Your outlook on life, who you develop relationships with, how you manage your finances, how you raise your kids, how you fight your spiritual battles, and how you believe God is a partition of the type of mindset you possess. Wrong thought patterns often lead to carnal mindsets. How you think ultimately determines how you live.

Let's take a deep dive into the different mindsets mentioned in the Bible, as referenced below.

"Types of Minds"

 ♦ *The Doubtful Mind*

"And seek not ye what ye shall eat, or what ye shall drink, neither be ye of <u>doubtful mind</u>," *(Luke 12:29).*

Doubt and dismay are rooted in fear. Having a mind filled with these type of thoughts is dangerous. These perspectives are often full of suspicion and distrust. Doubtful people will often say, "I think I believe you, but maybe I don't." This type of person wavers in their beliefs and lacks faith.

- ### *The Reprobate Mind*

  "And even as they did not like to retain God in their knowledge, God gave them up to a reprobate mind, to do those things which are not convenient," *(Romans 1:28)*.

  Individuals with this type of mindset will call evil good and good evil. They start losing the ability to discern right from wrong. The Scriptures and your conscious will no longer convict you. People with this type of thinking will believe a lie and start making excuses. They are uncorrectable, have itching ears, seeing God as an enemy, and will only strive to do things to please themselves. The Word of God is no longer final authority in this person's life.

- ### *The Willing Mind*

  "For if there first be a willing mind, it is accepted according to that a man hath, and not according to that he hath not," *(2 Corinthians 8:12)*.

  This type of individual is obedient and possesses a mind aligned with God's mind. They cheerfully consent to doing a certain task and have a vital core of compassion. They respect authority and are always ready to act.

◆ The Fleshly Mind

"Let no man beguile you of your reward in a voluntary humility and worshipping of angels, intruding into those things which he hath not seen, vainly puffed up by his <u>fleshly mind</u>," *(Colossians 2:18).*

A person with this type of thinking is focused on temporal and worldly pleasures. They lean more towards the secular side of life and sensual passions. They do not mind spiritual things and neglect deeper thought; they operate based on human nature and will not submit to God's law.

◆ The Sound Mind

"For God hath not given us the spirit of fear, but of power, and of love, and of a <u>sound mind,</u>" *(2 Timothy 1:7).*

A believer with this mind process possesses self-control and discipline. They seek scripture before making decisions and operate in good judgment. They rely on God's Spirit to do whatever God requires using wisdom and moving in clarity.

♦ *The Sober Mind*

"Young men likewise exhort to be <u>sober minded</u>," *(Titus 2:6).*

"Wherefore gird up the <u>loins of your mind, be sober</u>, and hope to the end for the grace that is to be brought unto you at the revelation of Jesus Christ," *(1 Peter 1:13).*

An individual with this mental state is alert and watchful of their surroundings. These type of persons can sense when something is off spiritually and recognize tactics of the enemy. They function calm, collected, having good sense and are level-headed during times of stress.

♦ *The Double Mind*

"A <u>double minded</u> man is unstable in all his ways," *(James 1:8).*

A person who struggles with this type of thinking is inconsistent. They will act one way today and another way tomorrow. Their desires change, as they pursue multiple things. Often, their loyalty is divided between God and the world. They are unstable and often can't make up their minds.

◆ *The Blind Mind*

"In whom we the God of this world hath <u>blinded the minds</u> of them which believe not, lest the light of the glorious gospel of Christ, who is the image of God, should shine unto them," *(2 Corinthians 4:4).*

This type of mindset is not helpful and finds it difficult to lead. A person possessing this thinking is lacking spiritual sight, often walking in darkness. They do not accept the things of God and are not spiritually discerned.

If you identify with any of these, you have power to accept or change your mental attitude. In Holiness, we want to move away from understanding and acting according to man's perspectives, and move towards acting according to God's perspective. It is time to change and renew your thoughts, shift your way of thinking. God is looking for people of faith. If you can change your thoughts, you can transform the world you live in. **The good news is that God gives us grace and guidance as we work out our own thinking.** This submission to a change of mind requires humility, patience and courage. **Everything starts with a thought, even a thought to change.**

A spirit-based mindset is willing, sober and sound. As believers, our strong belief in the Word of God should transform and reflect in our everyday reactions and behaviors. Our frame of reference and mindset through Scripture helps move us towards a particular set of Godly outcomes.

Is your mind totally consumed with the things of God? Is your conscious clean and your mind pure? This is a good thing! The mindset that God calls us to is one that is shaped by and in sync with His principles. Let's take a look at the spiritual mind as referenced throughout the Word, as seen below.

"Having One Mind"

- ◆ "Be of the same mind one toward another. Mind not high things, but condescend to men of low estate. Be not wise in your own conceits," *(Romans 12:16)*.
- ◆ "That ye may with one mind and one mouth glorify God, even the Father of our Lord Jesus Christ," *(Romans 15:6)*.
- ◆ "Only let your conversation be as it becometh the gospel of Christ: that whether I come and see you, or else be absent, I may hear of your affairs, that ye stand fast in one spirit, with one mind striving together for the faith of the gospel," *(Philippians 1:27)*.
- ◆ "For who hath known the mind of the Lord, that he may instruct him? But we have the mind of Christ," *(1 Corinthians 2:16)*.

In Scripture, we often see 'one mind' or 'one accord,' which means that we are unanimously linked with each other through the gospel. With respect and consideration of one another, we should agree about what should be done and think similar thoughts because we are all working together as a body of believers, following Christ's instruction.

Yet and still, we all have differing gifts according to the grace that is given to us. We are all members in one body, with one mind, yet we all *do not* have the same office (Rom. 12:4-7). God chooses who He wants to use for His glory. The priests lips keep knowledge, and we should always seek the law at his mouth for he is the messenger of the Lord of hosts (Mal. 2:7).

Our thoughts originate from the inside and the outside. Our *inner* thoughts can be compared to letters sent from our hearts *to the mind*. When we possess unclean, negative, or impure thinking, we need to ask God to create a clean heart inside and renew a right spirit within us (Psa. 51:10). Keeping the Word in our hearts helps to keep sin away and prevents any of our steps from sliding. Our steps are ordered, follow the path. "(11) Thy Word have I hid in my heart, that I might not sin against thee... (16) I will delight myself in thy statutes: I will not forget thy Word," (Psa. 119:11,16). The Word of God is living and active, it discerns our unspoken thoughts and suppressed intentions.

Do you harbor unforgiveness in your mind?

Would you tell us if you did?

Everyone has a story.

Everyone has been through something that changed them. Our love towards one another should flow from a pure heart, being of good conscience and of sincere faith. A spiritual-minded person can sense when God is not pleased. "Which shew the work of the law written in their hearts, their conscience also bearing witness, and their thoughts the mean while accusing or else excusing one another," (Rom. 2:15). *Unforgiveness* comes in many forms. It is most commonly defined as being unable or unwilling to forgive someone for hurting, betraying, or causing intense emotional pain. Having the mind of Christ will not allow you to be deceived. Having the mind of Christ will make it <u>impossible</u> to commit sin.

When trust is broken, for many it is hard to repair. However, God commands us to release any contempt, grudges or bitterness that seeks to fester and take root. When unforgiveness goes unchecked, it prevents blessings from flowing into our lives. "Then came Peter unto him, and said, Lord, how oft shall my brother sin against me, and I forgive him? Till seven times? Jesus saith unto him, I say not unto thee, until seven times: but, until seventy times seven," (Matt. 18:21-22). That is 490 times in one day! God commands us to forgive someone who has wronged us, no matter how we may feel.

We must release and let go of things that seek to corrupt our spirits, no matter how difficult or painful it may be. The kings throne is upheld by mercy. Clearing our mind of the old junk or mess that is piled up, releases sin from our hearts and allows us to let it go. *There is freedom found in forgiveness.* When you are watching your thoughts, you can overcome evil with good.

A spiritual-minded person will always win over their old habits, addictions and weaknesses. **God does everything good and bad, ultimately *for* our good.** He deals with our inner-man, developing the spirit. Despite setbacks and negative circumstances, He ultimately wants the best for us. Thoughts that enter from the outside, come through the gate of our ears and the gate of our eyes, then into the mind. We must ask God to circumcise our ears and anoint our eyes.

Our brain is a powerful instrument, and our thought options are diverse. Consider the state of your current mind and allow God to direct you to where you should be. Allow Him to change your perspective and program your thinking for the better. Be conscious and honest with God as He develops your inner man, and acknowledge the intricacies of your thoughts within. *Are you watching your thoughts?*

Today, many people seek after trends and watch the news or social media for information. Many want to gather together to party, to go back to life as usual, to get out of the house. Yet, be watchful of those who count it a pleasure to riot in the day time and are unable to cease from sin (2 Pet. 2:13-14). "Behold, the day is come, saith the Lord God, that I will send a famine in the land, not a famine of bread, nor a thirst for water, but of hearing the words of the Lord," (Amos 8:11).

It's time for the people of God to be alert and wake up out of sleep. **Capture every thought and turn the battle to the gate** (Isa. 28:6). The enemy knows he has a short time left. We must be on patrol day and night, guarding the gate of our minds. Be sober and seek God, as you prepare yourself to meet the Lord. The battle between the flesh and the spirit, angels and demons, good and evil continues to wage. We must stand watchful, discerning time and judgment.

"And beside this, giving all diligence, add to your faith virtue; and to virtue knowledge; and to knowledge temperance; and to temperance patience; and to patience godliness; and to godliness brotherly kindness; and to brotherly kindness charity. For if these things be in you, and abound, they make you that ye shall neither be barren nor unfruitful in the knowledge of our Lord Jesus Christ," (2 Peter 1:5-8).

The battle that rages between the flesh and the spirit is nothing compared to the everyday battle engaged in our own minds. We must be diligent in conquering our own thoughts and have wisdom to reflect on things pertaining to the spirit. We must keep

94

our minds **stayed** upon good works and Godly matters. Then, you will have peace to walk in the spirit and you will have good success (Josh. 1:8).

Commit your works to God and your thoughts will be established (Prov. 16:3). In doing these things, we can fulfill God's calling on our lives and live in peace. "Thou wilt keep him in perfect peace, whose mind is stayed on thee: because he trusteth in thee," (Isa. 26:3). We must not lean to our own understanding, but continue to acknowledge Him in all that we say, think, and do.

My Chapter Notes:

_____

_____

_____

_____

_____

Thought Watchers

Reference Scriptures:

Genesis 6:5	Romans 1:28
Exodus 30:12	Romans 2:15
Joshua 1:8	Romans 7:23-25
Psalm 40:5	Romans 8:5-6
Psalm 51:10	Romans 12:4-7
Psalm 91:10	Romans 15:6
Psalm 119:13	2 Corinthians 4:4
Proverbs 16:3	2 Corinthians 8:12
Proverbs 18:21	2 Corinthians 10:3-5
Proverbs 23:7	Ephesians 2:3
Isaiah 26:3	Ephesians 4:17-23
Isaiah 28:6	Philippians 1:27
Isaiah 65:17	Philippians 2:2-3, 5
Jeremiah 5:25	Philippians 3:19-20
Jeremiah 6:19	Philippians 4:8
Lamentations 3:21	Colossians 2:18
Ezekiel 11:5	Colossians 3:12-14
Amos 8:11	1 Thessalonians 4:11-12
Malachi 2:7	2 Thessalonians 2:2
Matthew 5:19	2 Timothy 1:7
Matthew 18:21-22	Titus 1:15
Mark 7:20	Titus 2:6
Luke 12:29	Hebrews 8:10
John 16:33	James 1:8

Reference Scriptures:

1 Peter 1:13

2 Peter 1:5-8

2 Peter 2:13-14

1 John 2:19

6 BROTHERS, BLOODLINES & THE BIRTHRIGHT

Can something exist without its opposite? That is a profound question that has puzzled Biblical scholars over decades. To imagine something going up and not down, or being hot and not cold is baffling, to say the least. How would peace be present if there was no chaos? What would life mean, if death did not exist?

Thought provoking questions, opposing ideas, and contrary concepts co-exist even today. For example, modern marketing strategies place competing businesses in close location to each other. According to a Cornell University article on Game theory and chain restaurants, this is why you will often see competing like-businesses such as McDonalds and Burger King, Walgreens and CVS, or Walmart and Target within blocks of each other. They have discovered that the best and most profitable location is when they are near each other. Here in this business strategy used in society, or in recognizing spiritual connections used in the Word of God, we can see how opposing relationships can also be mutually dependent on one another.

A famous concept introduced by respected astrologer, Dane Rudhyar states, "Everything is known through its opposite." Similarly, opposing yet complimentary forces can be seen throughout the Bible, whether in referencing Heaven and Earth, God and Satan, fire and water, light and darkness, **or the flesh and the spirit.**

Throughout Scripture, the fruits of the spirit are made contrast with the works of the flesh. In understanding these differing concepts, we learn how they are depicted in *familial* relationships as we go deeper in the Word of God. Often this conflict concerning family, generational bloodlines, and between brothers is actually a metaphorical paradox representing the flesh and the spirit.

First, we must understand the positive narrative about family in the Bible. Second, we will discover some foundational beliefs and values that are important in bonding with our loved ones and building Godly relationships. Then, we will look at conflict between family throughout Scripture and how this translates to important principles on the flesh and the spirit.

Family in the Bible

The concept of family is extremely important in Holiness, it was introduced in the beginning as an essential building block of creation

(Mk. 10:6-8). "And thy seed shall be as the dust of the Earth, and thou shalt spread abroad to the west, and to the east, and to the north, and to the south: and in thee and in thy seed shall all the families of the Earth be blessed," (Gen. 28:14).

Family is important to God. Family means to have someone love you unconditionally, in spite of your shortcomings. It is being the best person you can be so that you may inspire your loved ones. When these close relationships are built on a Godly foundation and developed properly, "family" means nobody gets left behind or forgotten. This close personal unit should help you develop traits and characteristics which reflect Christ, while seeking to impact your life spiritually and naturally for the good.

God gives us clear instructions on how we should treat each other and our family members, in the Scriptures below:

- "Honour thy father and thy mother: that thy days may be long upon the land which the Lord thy God giveth thee," (Ex. 20:12).
- "Train up a child in the way he should go: and when he is old, he will not depart from it," (Prov. 22:6).
- "Lo, children are an heritage from the Lord: and the fruit of the womb is his reward," (Psa. 127:3).
- "Submitting yourselves one to another in the fear of God. Wives submit yourselves unto your own husband,

as unto the Lord. For the husband is head of the wife, even as Christ is the head of the church: and He is the saviour of the body," (Eph. 5:21-23).

◆ "(25) Husbands, love your wives, even as Christ loved the church, and gave himself for it... (28) So ought men to love their wives as their own bodies. He that loveth his wife loveth himself. (29) For no man ever yet hated his own flesh...," (Eph. 5:24-29).

◆ "Children's children are the crown of old men; and the glory of children are their fathers," (Prov. 17:6).

◆ "What therefore God hath joined together, let no man put asunder," (Mk. 10:9).

◆ "Forbearing one another, and forgiving one another, if any man have a quarrel against any: even as Christ forgave you, so also do ye. And above all things put on charity, which is the bond of perfectness. And let the peace of God rule in your hearts, to the which also ye are called in one body; and be ye thankful," (Col. 3:13-15).

◆ "Behold, how good and pleasant it is for brethren to dwell together in unity," (Psa. 133:1).

◆ "Let love be without dissimulation. Abhor that which is evil; cleave to that which is good. Be kindly affectioned one to another with brotherly love; in honour preferring one another," (Rom. 12:9-10).

♦ "Let brotherly love continue," (Heb. 13:1).

Today, close family connections are still valued but scarce. Most families communicate distantly over the phone, social media, video chat, or the occasional reunion and outside barbecue. Many times only to congregate at weddings, child-events, graduations or during a ceremony of remembrance to honor a loved one who has passed. In the desire to 'do our own thing' or 'go our own way,' we often miss the importance and blessing that God desires family to bring into our lives. "Furthermore we have had fathers of our flesh which corrected us, and we gave them reverence: shall we not much rather be in subjection unto the Father of Spirits, and live?" (Heb. 12:9).

We have all heard the phrases, "Like father, like son" or "You have your mother's eyes." While physical characteristics we are born with may be hereditary, such as height, weight, hair, color, and complexion, which tend to run in families. **In the Kingdom of Heaven, the most important family connection is spiritual, not by blood or physical.** As the church, we are a part of the universal body of believers, adopted into the "family of God." When we are adopted into God's spiritual family, He becomes our Father. This spiritual group is not bound by ethnicity, gender, or social standing. We are all one body in Him.

This is why the term *"brother, brethren, or sister"* can be used to describe a person is various contexts, as seen below:

(1) A man (or woman) who have the same parents or one parent in common with another

(2) One related to another by common ties or interests

(3) A close friendship

(4) A fellow member

Our family, brothers or sisters, are not limited to our bloodlines. An encouraging nun, known as Mother Angelica is quoted saying, "A family spirit is not always synonymous with family life. Bone of our bone and flesh of our flesh makes for brothers, sisters and relatives, who may be as distant as strangers in a foreign land."

While family is not restricted to physical relation, it is also extended beyond today and can be represented in the future. God's power and influence has the ability to bring ***generational blessings*** – or curses – into our lives. Traditionally, when God bestows favor on *you*, that also includes your potential or forthcoming descendants. As in this instance with our forefather Abraham, God covered and blessed an entire generation. "That in blessing I will bless thee, and in multiplying I will multiply thy seed as the stars of the Heaven, and as the sand which is upon the sea shore; and thy seed shall possess the gate of his enemies; And in thy seed shall all the nations of the Earth be blessed; because thou hast obeyed my voice," (Gen. 22:17-18).

Your praise, prayers and obedience has the ability to bless your children, their children, your great grandchildren, and creations after them. Others will be impacted and affected by the decisions you make today. When God looks at you, He sees where you came from. Additionally, visualizing not just the individual you are today but the frontrunner of a generation. We can build a lifelong legacy by putting God first, earnestly serving Him, and asking Him to bless our families and our lives.

All the same, the Lord giveth and the Lord taketh away. Just as God can bless, He can also deny His covering and protection for our families and ourselves, as a consequence of sin or an action. A *generational curse* involves negative patterns from your family history, repeating and resurfacing in the lives of possibly you and future descendants. "Thou shalt not bow thyself to them, nor serve them: for I, the Lord thy God am a jealous God, visiting the iniquity of the fathers upon the children unto the third and fourth generation of them that hate me," (Ex. 20:5). These inherited burdens or afflictions can include unhealthy relationship habits, addiction, negative traits and more. "Our fathers have sinned, and are not; and we have borne their iniquities," (Lam. 5:7).

Family Conflict and Sibling Rivalry in the Bible

All of us are created as human agents of God. Sent forth with a purpose to complete, a mission to resolve, or an assignment to promote Christ's agenda. The people we get to help, the family we are born into, and the struggles we face are not by chance or by accident. Our devotion to God is revealed daily as He instructs, and directs us towards our destiny.

In the upcoming sections, we will discover how people and parables in the Bible, play a larger role in understanding the conflict between the flesh and the spirit. Each story will show the parallel between the spiritual characters in action and the spiritual conflict unseen. Recognizing this analogy or bigger picture, allows us to reflect and understand the daily battles that each of us face within our own lives, and how to overcome our desires through the Word of God.

The Spirit		**The Flesh**	
A	Abel	C	Cain
I	Isaac	I	Ishmael
J	Jacob	E	Esau
A	Abraham		
R	Rachel	L	Leah
S	Sarah	H	Hagar

"My Brother's Keeper: The Story of Cain & Abel"

In Chapter One, we discussed how Adam & Eve's disobedience in the garden created a curse over their family, their bloodline, and generations to come. As time passed, they endured new hardships. Being enlightened and now knowing good and evil, they reluctantly returned to tilling the ground and everyday living. "And Adam knew Eve his wife; and she conceived, and bare Cain, and said, I have gotten a man from the Lord, and she again bare his brother Abel..." (Gen. 4:1-2).

In one of the most infamous examples of sibling rivalry, Cain and Abel have been known for family scandal; as brothers involved in a depiction of lies, jealousy and murder. Cain was the firstborn, a farmer and a tiller of the ground. His younger brother, Abel was righteous and a keeper of the sheep. The twin brothers, each made sacrifices to God from his own labor. "(3)... Cain brought of the fruit of the ground an offering unto the Lord. (4) And Abel, he also brought of the firstlings of his flock and the fat thereof. And the Lord had respect unto Abel and to his offering: (5) But unto Cain and to his offering he had not respect. And Cain was very wroth, and his countenance fell," (Gen. 4:3-5).

Even though they both offered up sacrifice, God refused Cain's offering instead favoring Abel's gift. This illustration shows how we must give our best to God and offer Him that which is good continually. Be sincere when paying your tithes and give with goodwill an offering to His name. "Every man according as he purposeth in his heart, so let him give; not grudgingly, or of necessity: for God loveth a cheerful giver," (2 Cor. 9:7).

As the story continues on, an infuriated and jealous Cain lures Abel to a field to settle his wrath with an unexpected blow, striking him dead. With blood on his hands, Cain seemingly had no remorse in committing premeditated murderer of his own flesh and blood. "And the Lord said unto Cain, Where is Abel thy brother? And he said, I know not: Am I my brother's keeper?" (Gen. 4:9). Cain's response was disrespectful, dishonest, and snarky. In a sense, he was saying "My brother is not my problem."

Abel's blood cried out from the ground as if to testify of his deceit and wrongdoing. As a result, Cain was driven out of the land as a fugitive, exiled by God to the land of Nod. The ground no longer yielding him increase and sentenced to a life-time of wandering the Earth. "And Cain said unto the Lord, My punishment is greater than I can bear," (Gen. 4:13).

Abel was righteous and of the spirit, his life taken too soon by Cain's cruelty. Even though Cain was not merciful to His sibling, God *still* showed him mercy. In fear of being slain as ramification for his actions, God set a mark upon Cain to protect Him from anyone seeking vengeance to kill him. Cain later had his own family and a son, Enoch.

Today, small arguments and disagreements are common amongst siblings. Yet, Cain is a direct representation of operating in the flesh, his violence and sin brought him punishment and a disgraceful return. "They also that render evil for good are mine adversaries; because I follow the thing that good is," (Psa. 38:20). **We are all our brother's keeper.**

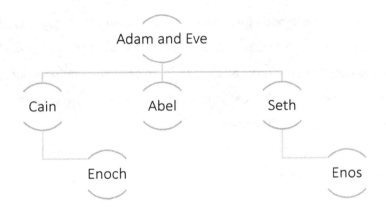

Do you know how powerful you are as a child of God? Yes. Then why do you fail to operate in that power? Every day we kill others with our mouths, by the words that we speak we become murderers (Prov. 18:21). Communicate righteously, speak life and not death! As a body of believers, when we fail to help our brother or sister, when we fail to give the firstfruits of our offering, or fail to show mercy we become like Cain. When we are covetous, we operate as children with no respect and no reverence. Exhibiting anger, violence, and bad character are carnal tendencies and traits of the flesh.

As Cain was sentenced to wander the Earth, similarly everywhere you go and everything you do will be hard when you do not put God first. When we are cruel and, in the flesh, we throw rocks at our brothers in Christ every day and hide our hand. Be determined to be kind. Show mercy. Give liberally. During this national pandemic, the church building may be closed but the true church is in you. "Forasmuch as ye are manifestly declared to be the epistle of Christ ministered by us, written not with ink, but with the Spirit of the living God; not in tables of stone, but in fleshly tables of the heart," (2 Cor. 3:3).

God will not receive the flesh. Jesus Christ has set us free! Let us praise Him and walk worthy of His grace and mercy. Fear not! God is a shield, and you are His child. "There shall no evil befall thee, neither shall any plague come nigh thy dwelling," (Psa. 91:10).

God will set His mark of protection upon you. He will give you everything that you need. "For it is God which worketh in you both to will and to do of His good pleasure. Do all things without murmuring and disputing," (Phil. 2:13-14). Trust Him! Have faith. Stay committed to righteousness as Abel, and be determined to walk in the Spirit.

"Blessed Bloodlines: God's Covenant with Abraham"

Abraham is a noble and significant depiction of righteousness in the Bible, revered as the first of the Hebrew patriarchs. He is a descendant of Noah and his humanity and work carries many titles. In fact, the Book of James refers to him as the "friend of God." Then, in Genesis it notes him as the "father of many nations" and in other accounts as the "father of the faithful." He is mostly known for his enduring obedience to God on his difficult journey of faith.

God's covenant rested with him and his descendants because of his steadfast devotion, willingness to seek God, and his wholehearted obedience. Kings would be born from his bloodline. Ultimately, God's plan to bring His gift of salvation to mankind through His Son, Jesus Christ, began with Abraham. The genealogy of Christ was established by God's covenant through him (Gal. 3:29).

"And I will make thee a great nation, and I will bless thee, and make thy name great: and thou shalt be a blessing. And I will bless them that bless thee, and curse him that curseth thee: and in thee shall all families of the Earth be blessed," (Gen. 12:2-3). Abraham believed God even though his wife Sarai couldn't have a child. He was childless and given an exceeding great promise of a son, and to be the father of nations, even in his old age.

Despite the promise, Sarai's flesh rises up and she moves ahead of God. "(1) Now Sarai Abram's wife bare him no children: and she had a handmaid, an Egyptian, whose name was Hagar. (2) And Sarai said unto Abram, Behold now, the Lord hath restrained me from bearing: I pray thee, go in unto my maid; it may be that I may obtain children by her. And Abram hearkened unto the voice of Sarai," (Gen. 16:1-3).

At 86 years old, Abraham became a father, and Hagar his wife's mistress (who she obliged him to marry) bare him a son, Ishmael. He was a wild man. God was a shield to Abraham and a great reward, despite his weakness. However, God still promised him a child from Sarai, saying that Ishmael was not his heir. God blessed Ishmael and promised to make him a great nation, but the covenant was with the son of Sarai. "For it is written, that Abraham had two sons, the one by a bondmaid, the other by a freewoman. But he who was of the bondwoman was born after the flesh: but he of the freewoman was by promise," (Gal. 4:22-23). Abraham and Sarai lived right. God blessed them, even leading God to change his name from Abram to Abraham, and his wife Sarai's soon after changed to Sarah, establishing a covenant with them. This covenant included circumcision of all the children in his generation. "Then Abraham fell on his face, and laughed, and said in his heart, shall a child be born unto him that is an hundred years old? And shall Sarah, that is ninety years old, bear?" (Gen. 17:17). **Is there anything too hard for God?**

Eventually, Abraham sent the bondwoman Hagar and his firstborn Ishmael away at Sarai's request. Right Away, Isaac became an only son. "(1) And it came to pass after these things, that God did tempt Abraham... (2) And he said, Take now thy son, thine only son Isaac, whom thou lovest, and get thee into the land of Moriah; and offer him there for a burnt offering upon one of the mountains which I will tell thee of," (Gen. 22:1-2). After worshipping, God tells Abraham to offer his only child, the son he had waited patiently for, as a sacrifice. In seeing his willingness to obey, God then provides a ram in the bush to save him from the heartbreak of killing his own son.

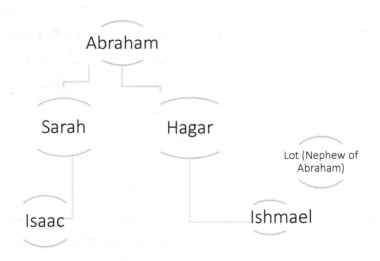

In this narrative, we see the contrast between Hagar and Ishmael of the flesh, and Sarah and Isaac of the spirit. Bless yourself by sowing to the spirit. Choose His Word! The spirit conquers everything. When God gets ready to open doors in our lives, He moves in a Heavenly space. "For we are His workmanship, created in

Christ Jesus unto good works, which God hath before ordained that we should walk in them," (Eph. 2:10).

Remember where God brought you from and be determined to believe Him. If He said it, that settles it! He knows when we truly believe Him and what is in our hearts. God tries each of us daily, just like Abraham was tried. Israel was afflicted for 400 years, as God was testing them. After you are tried, you will come forth as pure gold. Keep believing God. "If thou faint in the day of adversity, thy strength is small," (Prov. 24:10). Keep the faith and trust His Word. You will reap if you faint not.

There is a measure of faith and grace. Prove to yourself that you can pass this test. Whether the test is with family, faith, or finances. Nothing from nothing leaves nothing. Obey God in your giving and in your sacrifice to receive the promise. "That is, they which are the children of the flesh, these are not the children of God: but the children of the promise are counted for the seed," (Rom. 9:8). Prove to yourself that you can offer your best and operate in the Spirit. Every day God circumcises our hearts, compelling us to love Him and drawing us closer to Him. "(3) For what if some did not believe? Shall their unbelief make the faith of God without effect? (4) God forbid: yea, let God be true, but every man a liar..." (Rom. 3:3-4).

Ask God to draw you. There is no peace to the wicked. The relationship with Hagar (the flesh) produced the devil, a seed of unrighteousness. "This I say then, Walk in the Spirit, and ye shall not fulfill the lust of the flesh," (Gal. 5:16). Those that are in the flesh are not the children of God.

"Jacob Deceives Esau Out of His Birthright "

The war waged between the flesh and the spirit can cause peace and blessings, or conflict and broken families. The spirit will be submissive to the leading of God, the flesh will always try and go its own way. "We having the same spirit of faith, according as it is written, I believed, and therefore have I spoken; we also believe, and therefore speak," (2 Cor. 4:13).

In this example, we see twins wrestling for power from within the womb. "(22) And the children struggled together within [Rebekah]... (23) And the Lord said unto her, two nations are in thy womb, and two manner of people shall be separated from thy bowels; and the one people shall be stronger than the other people; and the elder shall serve the younger," (Gen. 25:22-23).

Isaac intended to give Esau a parental blessing. A *birthright* is defined as a particular right of possession or privilege one has from birth, especially as an eldest child. "And the boys grew: and Esau was a cunning hunter, a man of the field; and Jacob was a plain man, dwelling in tents," (Gen. 25:27). Esau was a skilled hunter and a man of the outdoor, he placed little value on his birthright, thinking more of his stomach than his soul. Jacob was a supplanter or deceiver, he disguised as his brother one night and stole his blessing. This one

116

action, triggering years of open hostility between the brothers. Esau associated himself with strange women, idolatry, and godlessness. Eventually, the brothers reconciled.

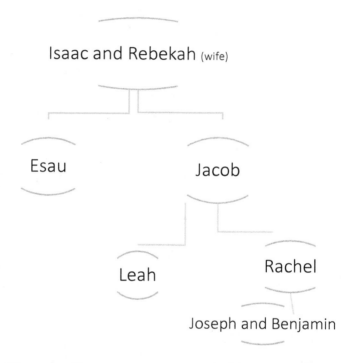

Isaac and Rebekah (wife)

Esau

Jacob

Leah

Rachel

Joseph and Benjamin

All of these families serve as a testament of the power of walking by faith and demonstrates the spirit conquering the flesh. We must crucify our flesh daily and cast aside "I" and the ego. "And they that are Christ's have crucified the flesh with the affections and lusts," (Gal. 5:24). Every man or woman bears their own burden, but every family an obligation of righteousness, in hope. *Like Abel, Abraham, Isaac, and Jacob of the promise– we are the children of God.*

Thought Watchers

My Chapter Notes:

_____

_____

_____

_____

_____

_____

Reference Scriptures:

Genesis 4:1-2, 3-5

Genesis 4:9, 13

Genesis 12:2-3

Genesis 16:1-3

Genesis 17:17

Genesis 22:1-2, 17-18

Genesis 25:22-23, 27

Genesis 28:14

Exodus 20:5, 12

Psalm 38:20

Psalm 91:10

Psalm 127:3

Psalm 133:1

Proverbs 17:6

Proverbs 18:21

Proverbs 22:6

Proverbs 24:10

Lamentations 5:7

Mark 10:6-8, 9

Romans 3:3-4

Romans 9:8

Romans 12:9-10

2 Corinthians 3:3

2 Corinthians 4:13

2 Corinthians 9:7

Galatians 3:29

Galatians 5:16, 24

Ephesians 2:10

Ephesians 5:21-23, 24-29

Philippians 2:13-14

Colossians 3:13-15

Hebrews 12:9

Hebrews 13:1

7 TEMPERATURE CHECK

Every day we are presented with choices. This morning, after rolling out of bed, taking a shower, and brushing your teeth you may have begun to pray and anticipate a great day. Continuing to comb your hair, then, sit for breakfast, pray and scroll online, you eventually decide to peek out of the blinds, trying to preview the weather conditions through the window.

Before deciding on an outfit, you flip on the screen, navigating to your favorite friendly meteorologist for specific climate updates. For some, you may have glanced at your phone app for the latest forecast predictions. Being inside and cozy, we plan and prepare for the changing outside conditions, checking the temperature to dress appropriately for a purposeful day.

This common example of a *temperature check* in the morning can be compared with how God assesses our inner-man. He examines our mind and hearts. Similarly, Scripture often references seasons or "temperature" changes; rain, heat, cold, burning, and even fire as metaphors for the flesh and the spirit. It is important to recognize the parallels between them and how they impact our walk

120

with God. "And in the morning, it will be foul weather to day: for the sky is red and lowring. O ye hypocrites, ye can discern the face of the sky; but can ye not discern the signs of the times?" (Matt. 16:3).

Weather warnings are important because they keep us prepared, protect lives, property and predict unexpected changes in the atmosphere. These tools calculate temperature patterns and atmospheric conditions. They also present important information that can affect our busy day to day timelines, schedules, and plans.

Serving God and participating in Kingdom-business should always be a priority. We serve God from our spirit. True submission and surrender to a Godly lifestyle comes from the inside. Our divine nature and professing Christ is all based on our reflection of His principles and walking in the knowledge of the Truth.

However, what happens when we feel like we are falling further and further away from God? When we attend services, clap our hands, pray, give an offering, follow leadership and do all the right things but something on the inside - *feels off*. **Are you truly serving God or are you just going through the motions? Are you desiring to know Him more or just doing all the right things?**

- "I know thy works, that thou art neither cold nor hot: I would thou wert cold or hot. So then because thou art lukewarm, and neither cold nor hot, I will spue thee out of my mouth," **(Rev. 3:15-16).**

Serving God is a lifestyle. It takes humility and a God-conscious mindset to serve God and others. A good leader and a true disciple will have the courage to follow when stakes are high, and faithfulness is costly. We must choose not to walk according to the prince of the power of the air (Eph. 2:2). When we choose to live our lives for Christ, we have an intentional mindset by God's grace against the misdirection of the world and our flesh.

Being in the Spirit of God determines how we think, how we spend our resources, time, talent, treasures and focus. "For God is my witness, whom I serve with the Spirit in the gospel of His Son..." (Rom. 1:9). It is difficult to serve leadership when you are functioning in the flesh. Your decisions will be contrary, you feelings overpowered with unrest, and everything will seem out of order. Our praise, giving, and mindset can be impacted by the condition of our hearts. "No man can serve two masters: for either he will hate the one, and love the other; or else he will hold to the one, and despise the other. Ye cannot serve God and mammon," (Matt. 6:24).

We should be content but never satisfied in serving God. **When we think we are doing the most, we should remind ourselves that we could always be doing more.** It should vex our Spirit when the House of God is out of order, when His people are out of place, when the sheep have gone astray. In times when we feel our spiritual temperature fizzling out, seek leadership on how to get back to the old path (Jer. 6:16).

122

Why does Jesus associate His disciples with these extreme temperatures, like hot or cold, and looms to discard them? Looking closer into Revelations 3:15-16, we see that He associates a weak-willed and shaky connection with Him as being "lukewarm." This means a believer's commitment to their spiritual purpose is being neglected. This passage serves as a wake-up call or *temperature check* to all of us; united as born-again, Holy Ghost speaking, faith-filled believers in the House of God, we must refresh the Spirit of God on the inside. It is a spiritual call to energize, awaken, rekindle, and recommit to our spiritual purpose.

For some, this national time of pause has drawn you closer to Him. For others, it has pushed you further and further away. It is dangerous to be lukewarm as a believer. All of us should want to be MORE than an 'ordinary servant.' We should pursue excellence, cease from making excuses, and commit to the cause. As a thought watcher, you must persevere despite obstacles and be committed to helping someone else.

Nothing escapes God's attention. **Lukewarm** is defined as lacking in conviction, being fickle, half-hearted, on the fence or unsettled. A person in this fleshly state operates as if in-a-dilemma, they are indecisive, and you can tell their hearts are not in it. In fact, according to God they are not *hot enough* or *cold enough* to be enjoyable. In a sense, He is telling His people to pick a side.

Do you like your meals at dinner to be room-temperature? No. You heat them back up until a desired heat or temperature is reached. Yes! It's the same plate of food at various temperatures, but eating it warm just isn't as satisfying. *How about your bath water? Or your coffee? Have you tasted lukewarm soda that has lost its fizz?* Exactly. None of those mentions are enjoyable at the wrong temperature. This state of *"melancholy measure"* is an indication of being "in-between," the "almost." Hot water could heal, Cold water could refresh. In context, Jesus is saying any decision is better than indecision.

Are we compromising in life and ministry? Is there more that we could be doing? We must be attentive not to simply continue to perform meaningless activities, offer visitors lifeless handshakes, going through the motions with an indifferent mindset. God would rather us be completely cold, at least in a position where change can happen; then having enough Word, enough knowledge of God, enough Scripture, but not being fully engaged nor operating in real faith. A Godly leader must have both – the courage to take people to a daring destination and the humility to selflessly serve others on the journey. "And if it seem evil to you to serve the Lord, choose this day whom you will serve; whether the gods which your fathers served that were on the other side of the flood, or the gods of the Amorites, in whose land ye dwell: but as for me and my house, we will serve the Lord," (Josh. 24:15).

God has given us a brain and reasoning capacity, but the fear of the Lord is the beginning of wisdom. Set your priorities in order and seek His presence. You can spiritually take your temperature according to your willingness to worship God, your willingness to seek His presence, your willingness to give and help, also your desire to serve Him wholeheartedly. Our external value is little in comparison to the unbelievable richness in Spirit, when obeying the words of God.

God-honoring leaders learn to look at life through God's eyes and not merely their own, because they realize their perspective is limited. True servants grow to honor Him as humility becomes a daily mindset and practice. God is mindful of those who have remained faithful in difficult times. A servant's heart should be meek and full of reverence. **Whether we are giving back our time, our finances, or our gifts – a thought watcher is aware that we are only giving God back what He has already given us.** He gave us life, thus giving us the time to serve Him and help in ministry. He is our source and the giver of all things; thus our money _comes from_ and _belongs to_ Him. He is our Creator, therefore any gifts and talents we have, He ultimately gave. Giving back is a key component in the mind and heart of a servant. A true thought watcher loves to serve!

In this next section, we will evaluate the climate of 'the church,' the pressures of 'the world,' and the condition of our hearts and minds. In understanding these concepts better, we can clearly identify which one represents the flesh and which one represents the spirit.

"Cold"

The state of being *cold* is synonymous with being chilly, crisp, frigid, being bitter, frosty, glacial or even icy. "And because iniquity shall abound, the love of many shall wax cold," (Matt. 24:12).

If the climate of your heart has grown cold, you can reconnect with God today. *How?* You can start by talking to Him. Listening to His voice and obeying His instruction. You can show gratitude for the little and big things. You can be mindful of His presence in your life, even when the pressures of this world can seem unbearable.

We can't share the love of Christ out of a cold, hardened heart. However, there will be a remnant who will not lose their love, during loss. There will be a remnant who will not lose their hope during national crisis. Their love of God during worldly loss will remain fixed, even strengthened.

In these dark and dangerous times, there will be a remnant that will stand firm and serve Him, in spite of. In spite of, sickness and disease. In spite of, lies and persecution. In spite of, heartache and pain. In spite of, financial hardship and lack. This remnant is a special and chosen group of people, who remain committed to the vision and remain committed to leadership in difficult times.

"Hot"

We can get so busy in our day to day lives that our fire for God starts to dwindle. Our hearts and soul will never be satisfied, until Jesus is our priority. When He fills you up, you will never want anything else. Nothing else compares to the love of Jesus. Allow the Holy Spirit to change you from your deepest parts. **When you ask God to set your heart on fire for Him, you are asking Him to make you passionate about what you do, to consume you from the inside-out.**

Rekindle your faith to burn for Jesus! Ask God to develop your inner-man and ask Him to allow you to become *more than* an ordinary servant. Check the temperature of your heart when serving leadership and be sure to follow Godly instruction. "(1) Let every soul be subject unto the higher powers. For there is no power but of God: the powers that be are ordained of God. (2) Whosoever therefore resisteth the power, resisteth the ordinance of God: and they that resist shall receive to themselves damnation. (3) For rulers are not a terror to good works, but to the evil. Wilt thou then not be afraid of the power? Do that which is good, and thou shalt have praise of the same: (4) For he is the minister of God to thee for good. But if thou do that which is evil, be afraid; for he beareth not the sword in vain: for he is the minister of God, a revenger to execute wrath upon Him that doeth evil," (Rom. 13:1-4).

Ask Him to set a fire down in your soul, in that your enthusiasm and love for Him cannot be contained. Your Spirit should be crying out in desperation and out of your 'belly' you should be declaring, "I want more of you God." With tears in your eyes and your hands lifted, allow His presence to re-ignite a passion for His House, His Word, and His people. God called us to be in community, gathering as coals together in a fire pit – on fire for Him. "And they said one to another, Did not our heart burn within us, while He walked with us by the way, and while He opened to us the scriptures," (Lk. 24:32).

In order to be *more than* an ordinary servant, we have a mandate to keep our fire for the Lord *hot* no matter the spiritual climate around us. "Not being slothful in business; fervent in spirit; serving the Lord," (Rom. 12:11). Remember when you would hungrily search the Scriptures for the voice of the Lord within the pages? Remember when you would put post-it notes all around your house, spending hours in the Word? Remember when you would come into the sanctuary when no one was there to praise or pray to God? Spending time in prayer is spending time in the presence of God. The presence of God is the air that our souls need to be on fire for Him. "Quench not the Spirit," (1 Thess. 5:19).

Spiritual passion is ignited when it is being used to serve others. Start using the gifts and talents that God has given you to help others and help the ministry (Matt. 25:14). Never underestimate the difference you can make in the lives of others and the impact you can make in the House of God. To give happiness to others is a great act of charity. There is no greater joy than being an instrument of the Holy Spirit. There is no greater joy than walking in the conviction and calling of God. There is no greater joy than helping someone in need. "That your faith should not stand in the wisdom of men, but in the power of God," (1 Cor. 2:5). Have faith that God can use your smallest gift and most insignificant talent for His glory. Every believer has something to offer God and you are no exception.

How to Stay on Fire for God:

- ♦ Feed the flames with the Word of God
- ♦ Stoke the Furnace with Prayer
- ♦ Worship the Lord with Extravagance
- ♦ Allow the Holy Spirit to Move
- ♦ Do a Spring Cleaning of your Heart
- ♦ Bring Your Flame Closer to Other Flames
- ♦ Start Making Your Fire Useful

     ~ Article Reference: Taber, Viral Believer

While this helps us to better understand the concept of hot, cold, and lukewarm in this passage. Let's take a look further into the text. "...I will spue thee out of my mouth," is a potent and powerful statement. Spue (or spew) is defined as expelling something rapidly and forcibly. It is to discharge, emit, gush, pour, or eject from the stomach. All intents and purposes, it means to vomit. When there is something in your life that you do not want to absorb, inhale, or ingest, your body will naturally reject it. It is a signal of disgust and a reflex of displeasure. "They were all ashamed of a people that could not profit them, not be an help nor profit, but a shame, and also a reproach," (Isa. 30:5). None of us want to be a shame to the Lord, none of us want to make Him sick.

In today's culture, it's often a me-first mentality, a willingness to serve is not a popular concept. The world defines greatness by power, prestige, possessions, and position. Yet even, Boxer Muhammad Ali once said, "Service to others is the rent you pay for your room here on Earth." **We serve God by serving others. A person's most useful asset is not a head full of knowledge, but a heart full of love, an ear ready to listen, and a hand willing to help.**

Stir up your pure minds by way of remembrance. Refresh the God in you. We must operate in the will of God. Hear the conclusion of the whole matter and muse (meditate) on the Lord. Examine yourself and check your spiritual temperature today. Serve Him with your whole heart. Let your dreams live. You were created for good works. Make the decision to walk and do good, serve and be happy, help and give generously. As long as you stay close to God and never give up, He will stay close to you. As long as you continue to seek the Lord, He will make you to prosper (2 Chron. 26:5).

My Chapter Notes:

_____

_____

_____

_____

_____

_____

Thought Watchers

Reference Scriptures:

Joshua 24:15

2 Chronicles 26:5

Isaiah 30:5

Jeremiah 6:16

Matthew 6:24

Matthew 16:3

Matthew 24:12

Matthew 25:14

Luke 24:32

Romans 1:9

Romans 12:11

Romans 13:1-4

1 Corinthians 2:5

Ephesians 2:2

1 Thessalonians 5:19

Revelations 3:15-16

Bishop M.B. Jefferson

8 GOOD HABITS

The Bible is a roadmap to a meaningful life. In pursuit of Heaven, not only do we need to receive salvation, but maintain deliverance over the works of the flesh. The wisdom to maintain the thoughts of God and to function in the Spirit of God, requires a sound mind and good habits. Our desire should be to have a deeper relationship with Him, ask Him to know the secret places inside of you. To make manifest what is limiting your potential in Him. To help you overcome hindering or self-destructive tendencies.

A person can fall into unhealthy patterns that can lead them into sin and immoral thinking, or on the contrary, cultivate behaviors that contribute to victorious living. Your habits are either empowering you to achieve victory and succeed, or preventing and holding you back. For most of us, the state and quality of our lives is a direct reflection of the habits that we possess. Good habits are going to propel you forward while pesky bad habits are going to hold you back. "For which cause we faint not; but though our outward man perish, yet the inward man is renewed day by day," (2 Cor. 4:16).

To make better life choices, we need to constantly be aware of what we are thinking. Our common place rituals, whether it be prayer in the morning, fasting until noon, listening to praise music in the car, or exercising after work all become a part of us. Likewise, what we think, what we say, and what we do are all controlled by the habits that we possess. Several studies suggest that our behaviors account for <u>nearly half</u> of all of our actions. **Not only do we need to build good habits, but we need to build God habits.**

The goal is to consciously be aware of both good and bad thoughts, which are a root cause of both good and bad actions. Take heed to watch your thoughts. All habits that pertain to life and Godliness will be aligned with the Word of God. Fight the good fight of faith to disrupt your bad habits, be mindful not to give a way for the enemies tactics and deceit. Keep fighting for your deliverance, keep fighting for your freedom. "Fight the good fight of faith, lay hold on eternal life, whereunto thou art also called, and hast professed a good profession before many witnesses," (1 Tim. 6:12).

While good habits in the natural include: eating healthy foods, brushing twice a day, cleaning up our mess, being polite, having table manners, and practicing gratitude. Bad habits can include oversleeping, smoking, procrastinating, negative self-talk, nail biting, and overeating. "So then they that are in the flesh cannot please God," (Rom. 8:8). Stop procrastinating about all those things you say you want to do but never get around to doing. Today, you can make the decision to break a bad habit by replacing it with a good one.

Most of us need structure and routine in our lives. However, to get ahead we must attempt to overlook the *unimportant things* that waste time but that we tend to fixate over. Focus on the spiritual elements that can improve our everyday living, and not just the natural. *Think God.*

Our thoughts become our words. Our words become our actions. Our actions become our habits. Our habits turn into our values and character. To sum up, our values and character can create our destiny. **Do you know the character of God?** He is mighty and good. Take heart in your struggles, God sees and knows of you. Think and meditate on who He is in His Word. He will make Himself known to you. He wants to help you and lead you into total deliverance.

Good Spiritual Habits

♦ Make Morning Prayer a Priority

If you have allowed anxious thoughts to "set up shop" in your mind the moment you open your eyes, change your morning energy by entering into a state of prayer and praise. Thank God in advance for providing you with the stamina, protection, and grace to get through all the day's demands by making prayer a priority.

♦ **Study and Devote Time to God**

Commit to reading at least one Scripture or a daily devotion in the morning. This time of devotion will set your thoughts in the right direction. Studying helps set a positive tone for your entire day and gives you the opportunity to learn more about Christ. Show God your obedience by putting Him before everything else in your life.

♦ **Listen to Praise and Worship Music**

The habit of listening to music that glorifies God will uplift you and compels you to be more Kingdom-focused every day. It also provides a much needed break from the worries and cares of this world.

♦ **Meditate on the Scriptures**

Smiling and reading the Word of God is the great source of peace. Take an inventory of your thoughts. *Adjust, and begin to think about what you have been thinking about.* You have authority over your own thoughts and power to reject any thought that doesn't line up with what God says about you.

◆ Talk to God throughout the Day

The 60 second prayer is a helpful way to overcome the negative habit of grumbling and complaining. When you are tempted to voice your criticism, replace it with talking to God about how thankful you are. The more we talk to God, the less we complain. There is no way you can complain while giving thanks for His grace, and no way you can protest while praising Him for His provision. The habit of setting our thoughts on the positive, requires taking our focus off what we don't like. Then, putting our focus on giving Him the glory that He deserves.

It takes practice to develop spiritual habits over a lifetime. When adopted, transformation and lasting changes take effect. "In your patience possess ye your souls," (Lk. 21:19). Until you become sincere and admit your areas of weakness, you will struggle with ungodly thoughts. **Until you make a decision to consistently obey the Scriptures, sin can resurface in your life.** Obedience is an expression of the basic principle that God is the Creator and designer of the universe. He loves us and therefore His counsel and His commandments can be trusted. Build your foundation on this principle. If the foundation be destroyed, what can the righteous do?

Thought watchers develop Godly habits. Be patient with yourself, trust God to step in and guide you. He cares for your well-being and the state of your soul. Many people are depressed and unhappy because they are attempting to live in a way that contradicts the design and intention of God. Build the right bridge towards Him, by overcoming the works of the flesh. **Be intentional about establishing _good_ Godly habits in your life.**

It is impossible for sin to co-exist in the heart of someone who truly watches their thoughts. The Scriptures cannot be broken, yet people break the commandments every day. The moment we let our thoughts run rampant, we begin a dangerous journey into the dark. Do not deceive your own selves, bad habits can fester and contaminate our core. Sin is like drinking poison and expecting your soul to prosper. "But fornication, and all uncleanness, or covetousness, let it not be once names among you, as becometh saints; neither filthiness, nor foolish talking, nor jesting, which are not convenient: but rather giving of thanks. For this ye know that no whoremonger, nor unclean person, nor covetous man, who is an idolater, hath any inheritance in the Kingdom of Christ and of God," (Eph. 5:3-5).

Possessing Godly communication is important characteristic of a thought watcher. If our words create our thoughts, than our words need to give life. "I said, I will take heed to my ways, that I sin not with my tongue: I will keep my mouth with a bridle, while the wicked is before me," (Psa. 39:1). The ability to hold your peace, requires you to watch what you want to say. The communication that we speak, can be a help or a hindrance in the thoughts that we sow, into the mind of someone else. A word spoken travels from your lips to their ears, from their ears to their minds. That is why the Scripture tells us that death and life are in the power of the tongue.

"But sanctify the Lord God in your hearts: and be ready always to give an answer to every man that asketh you a reason of the hope that is in you with meekness and fear, having a good conscience; that, whereas they speak evil of you, as of evildoers, they may be ashamed that falsely accuse your good conversation in Christ," (1 Pet. 3:15-16). It is better that we suffer for well doing than for evil.

Sound speech and effectual communication is mentioned over and over in the Bible. Your thoughts and your words have power. You are snared by the words of your own mouth. You can speak life or kill your own blessings. You can give someone hope or kill their dreams. You can uplift and inspire, or discourage and condemn. You can think God or think on things of the world. "Behold, I stand at the door, and knock: if any man hear my voice, and open the door, I will come in to him, and sup with him, and he with me," (Rev. 3:20). Ask yourself: "Who is knocking at the gates of my mind?"

Good habits, clean hands, sound speech, a willing mind, and a pure heart is what God desires. The King of Glory is strong and mighty in battle. He can help you to overcome the flesh and walk in the Spirit. God Almighty can help you watch your thoughts. Seek the Lord before you let a word utter from your lips. Seek the Lord before you make a decision or think a thought. Seek the Lord as you serve in His House and direct your families (Psa. 24).

We all want to make it into the Kingdom of Heaven. Develop Holy habits that will help you make it through the gate on that glorious day! Surround yourself with people who want to live the way you want to live. Cut out as many triggers as possible. Eliminate those things that prevent you from attaining a better life for yourself. God will give you the grace to not give up.

Real change is not overnight. Yet, God can work miracles in your life if you let Him into your heart today. Let Him into your mind. **God can change the spiritual world you live in, if you will make a decision to change your natural thinking.** Watch your ideas and reflections; think positive! Don't give up on God because He won't give up on you. *He's able!*

My Chapter Notes:

_____

_____

_____

_____

_____

_____

Reference Scriptures:

Psalm 24

Psalm 39:1

Luke 21:19

Romans 8:8

2 Corinthians 4:16

Ephesians 5:3-5

1 Timothy 6:12

1 Peter 3:15-16

Revelation 3:20

Bishop M.B. Jefferson

CONCLUSION

A thought-watcher recognizes the vital role that our thoughts play in predicating our actions. **What you allow into your mind can cause you to walk in victory or live in defeat.** Through the Word of God, we program out mind for next-level thinking. We can program our mind to operate in the Spirit of God, where love, joy, peace, longsuffering, gentleness, faith, meekness and temperance dwell.

Breakthrough thinking is based on sound doctrine. Uploading the correct information into our spirit-man shifts our perspective to reflect the thinking of Christ. In order to do the impossible, we must first widen our thinking. In order to be spiritual minded, we must cast down thoughts that pertain to the flesh. We can apply good habits to help us in practical ways, as we pursue the mind of Christ.

Where the Spirit of the Lord is, there is liberty. Challenge yourself daily, immerse yourself in the Word of God. Our thoughts shape who we are and who we can become. Watch the gate of your ear and eyes to protect what enters your mind. The human brain weighs only about three pounds, but it is the control center of the entire body. A Godly mindset is powerful. What you think about yourself on the inside is what you will manifest on the outside.

Through these pages, we have journeyed through my life story. I pray my testimony positively impacts your life and helps you to change for the better. When the enemy comes in like a flood, you must set up a standard in your mind (Isa. 59:19). Choose who you will think on in times of turmoil. Choose who you will think on in times of prosperity.

Through God's grace and deliverance, He has given me wisdom. We must be word-conscious and constantly think on God. Yes, we should always 'thank God,' but additionally we should also "think God." Seeing life through His viewpoint allows us to fix our minds, it allows us to understand the mysteries of the Kingdom of Heaven. God can deliver you from whatever you are going through today. Miracles today and in times past, are a result of directing our minds and hearts towards victorious living. Set a standard in your life, resist the enemies tactics and allow good to flow into your life.

The fear of the Lord is the beginning of wisdom. A Godly mindset allows us to understand the direction and the will of the Lord. Overcome the flesh by developing the inner-man, in doing this your stumbling blocks can become your stepping stones. Your trials can become your testimony. Your mistakes can become milestones of wisdom to share. Ultimately, your thoughts will translate into your destiny. Who you are, who you can be, and who you are destined to become all begin by having the mind of Christ.

ABOUT THE AUTHOR

BISHOP M.B. JEFFERSON is an innovative leader and an instrumental asset to the Body of Christ. With his fiery testimony and prophetic gifting, he has influenced a worldwide awakening for truth. Through messages of Holiness, Bishop Jefferson impacts the lives of thousands of individuals across the globe – *calling for a change*. Along with his wife, Dr. Brenda Jefferson, they are founders and senior pastors of Living in Victory Christian Church, The House of David Help Center, and World Assemblies Fellowship International.

Over forty plus year in ministry, Bishop M.B. Jefferson and Dr. Brenda Jefferson have remained faithful to the call of God on their lives. Through Scripture-based teachings, they uniquely point believers and non-believers alike toward the cross, teaching love, judgment, kindness and the detrimental effects of addiction and sin.

146

Bishop M.B. Jefferson

OTHER WORKS BY BISHOP JEFFERSON

BOOKS:

LIVING IN VICTORY

CHANGE YOUR THOUGHTS, CHANGE YOUR WORLD

TRANSFORMATION OF THE MIND

BEGGING TO BE DELIVERED

THE 50 LIST

I GOT IT

VISIT BISHOP M.B. JEFFERSON ONLINE:

www.mbjefferson.org

www.livcc.org